Distributed by Reunion Books
3949 Old State Road 446
Bloomington, IN 47401

Printed by World Arts Inc.
156 E. Franklin St.
Spencer, IN 47460

ISBN 0-9619795-9-3

Unless otherwise specified, all persons named
herein are real, all their stories are true.

To My Wife

MARION

Who Makes Everything Possible

" . . . ye are of more value than many sparrows.

— *Matt. 10:31*

CONTENTS

TURNING POINT

Often an insignificant incident may be the turning point of an individual's life. This story that follows substantiates that small events may be the cross-roads of your life. It was told by Morris R. Graves, 6291 W. SR 48, Bloomington, IN.

I was six; Mother decided that I should start to school. She was influenced probably by the character and charm of the teacher assigned to Center School, our district.

With new Primer, Golden Rod Tablet, and a lunch pail, I started toward school, one and a quarter miles east of home. As I sauntered along, my imagination wandered on this September morning. Could bears or Indians be lurking in Abe Weimer's woods? Were the people in the Weimer house watching me? Were snakes hiding as I crossed little Indian Creek? Could robbers be using the quarry hole by Phillips' Lane? Will all the kids laugh at me, a green kid?

With great show of bravery, I climbed the wooded slope to the Center School, where the teacher gave me a little desk at the front of room. I moseyed to the window and observed the children on the playground; many appeared so big; young, vigorous men. Those fifteen year old guys were so boisterous and rough act-ing that I had horrors of what might befall a little boy should their whims or wrath be incurred.

The toilets, two giant four-holers, were located at opposite corners of the school lot, the boys' toilet on the northwest corner. As I watched the play, the big boys seemed to prefer wrestling, jumping, et cetera, by the path which led to the boys' toilet. I sensed dan-ger! Jumping into a lion's den made as much sense as passing those "big boys" to reach the toilet.

Holding one's water from 8:30 a.m. until 4:00 p.m.,

the time school was dismissed, caused great pain and demanded diligent attention to restrain the surging tide. The first day of school was miserable; so was the second.

On the third day after the last recess, my resistance became exhausted; nature's process could be denied no further. Water ran in a stream from my little desk, near the front; it followed over pine board flooring to the rear of the house. Of course, this was no experiment to prove the house was not level, but nevertheless water seeking its level showed definitely that the building sloped toward the south — rear — of the room.

As the liquid gently coursed along the pine flooring, pupils were giggling and pointing in my direction. The red-faced, much embarrassed, young lady teacher pretended nothing unusual was happening.

I was so embarrassed and humiliated. I thought the whole world knew or would learn of my accident. Of course, the world would treat me harshly. I would be treated as inferior and ostracised. At the moment, death would have been welcome; in my deep depression, I received little satisfaction from my great physical relief.

If my teacher had been trained in modern psychology, I am sure she would have shown compassion and reassured me that accidents happen to most little boys — even the best — and the world soon forgets trivial episodes; or she could have led me to believe that I was a glamorous, exciting first-grader, but this did not occur. My good teacher let me go home ashamed of myself. Wetting my pants and becoming completely mortified was, no doubt, the most important crisis of my life.

Coming from school, sobbing and relating my woes, I approached Mother. Lovingly, Mother held her youngster in a tight embrace for comfort only a mother can give.

I, only six years, knew the compulsory school attendance law was from seven to sixteen years. With this knowledge, I asked Mother to please let me stay home; I didn't wish to go before I was seven. Mother consented so I delayed school another year. This delay, caused by wetting my pants, changed my life and the lives of several people. If I had continued school at age six, I would have graduated from eighth grade one year before school bus service began in Indian Creek Township, where we lived. Without bus service, I would not have been able to go to high school, to become the first male descendent of Peter Graves, Jr. to receive a high school diploma. I would not have gone to college; I could not have taught school; neither could I have passed a civil service test sufficiently high for employment. As may be determined, wetting my britches was no disaster but indirectly it changed my future.

Even my marriage was a result of this accident. I rode the school bus with Lois Mood and courted her through high school. Without that relationship, the probability is great that we never would have married.

Today, I testify: "Wetting my britches was the most important crisis of my life."

BIRTHRIGHT

Unless sheriff Joe Gee decided after reading this to toss him in the clink, Clyde Hawkins of Shoals had never been in jail.   Not in his whole life, and that's one more year than man's allotted three score and ten.   Except for two times, however.

The first time was as a juvenile, back on July 19, 1926. He popped in there when Old Doc Freeman delivered him to his mother, Grace.

"Well," you might like to ask, "what in the world was his mother doing in jail? Had she been arrested and incarcerated?"

Well, go ahead and ask. Everyone else does when they learn he was born in that Martin County institution.

Grace Hawkins had as good a reason as anyone for being in jail.   She was the wife of James Grover Hawkins, Clyde's father, who was sheriff at that time. Sheriffs served two-year terms then, and Grover — he was always addressed by his middle name — was sheriff during the years 1925 and 1926.

Grover and Grace had nine children, and although Clyde was the only one born in the jail, all but one of the others lived at the jail.

The second time Clyde was in jail was in 1970, when he himself was elected Martin County sheriff. His wife, Helen, and three of their four children also made their home there. It was the same old jail in which Clyde was born, and it got just as noisy for him and Helen and their family as it had when his father was sheriff.   On Saturday nights two cells on the upper floor and four on the lower floor were sometimes packed with as many as fifteen inmates. Usually drunks.   It got scary at times, and it wasn't unusual for Clyde and Helen to be awakened during

4

the night by one of the kids jumping in bed with them. Those were tough days. The money was skimpy, and with three kids in school the living wasn't easy. With only one full-time deputy, Clyde had to work around the clock. No days off. No vacation. The sheriff or his deputy was in demand at all hours.

By comparison, Joe Gee had five full-time deputies and a jail staff. They worked eight-hour shifts, had time off, vacations, benefits, and, something Clyde and his father before him would have liked to have had — a modern jail.

"There was a fireplace in every room," Clyde remembered the primitive living conditions, "and two coal stoves to heat the jail."

I found Clyde one morning in the kitchenette of the Hawkins home. When Helen opened the front door to my thumb on the doorbell I heard him call out to me from inside, "C'mon back here."

The kitchenette was at the opposite side of the house from the front door and he was seated there shuffling some papers. Windows there overlooked Water Street, and beyond that the waters of the East Fork of White River. Seated across from him for an hour turned out to be a comfortable experience.

Had I started for Shoals a little earlier that morning I might have found him at RJ's, a popular gas, coffee and conversation fill-up at the junction of US 50 and SR 150. He had walked there from home. For him it was a frequent pleasure to visit with old friends there, including Wayne Wade, Son Sorrells, George Lindsey, Herb Sherfick, Rex Baker, Wes Cooper and Bill Lee. But by the time I arrived at RJ's he had struck out for home.

The papers he had shuffled pertained to land acquisition. Before he became sheriff that is what he did for the state highway department. At that time it didn't pay too well and he got himself elected sheriff. During his tenure the money got better in the highway department and Clyde resigned his position and returned to work there.   At sixty-six he had retired from INDOT and was at this time self-employed, making studies of rights of way and land acquisitions for consulting engineering firms.

"I can't just sit around," he said. "I have got to be doing something and I can do this work at home. I want to keep active so I guess I'll continue to work as long as I am able. "

As a sheriff, as a county councilman, and especially as a person, Clyde had made many friends. He offered this suggestion for anyone who would enjoy such good fortune: "It's easier to smile than it is to frown," he said.

In a few words — those of his daughter Lynn Jones — "He's a great guy."

She had spoken to me about her father on an earlier occasion, informing me at the time that his birthplace was the old Martin County jail.

"To my knowledge," Clyde said, "no one else has ever been born there."

The old jail is gone now, but that unique bit of Martin County history lived on in Clyde, and his children, grandchildren and great grandchildren.   And now, thanks to Lynn, we have shared in it.

THE HUNT

We were looking for Bigfoot.

You could feel the tension from the back seat on your neck when Junior Tharpe leaned in the car window and said, "Sure I saw Bigfoot." And it seemed for good measure he added with emphasis, "Several times."

Nancy, on the front seat between Marion and me, seemed to stiffen a little. Junior wasn't joking. His face was as straight as a die, no giveaway or surreptitious smile. No corn-eating possum grin.

"The first time was one morning when I was walking to the school bus stop," he said.

Also, Bernard Gallagher hadn't made a mistake. He knew what he was talking about when earlier he had waved a hand toward the fork in the road and told us, "Take a sharp right there and go on about a half mile and you'll be in Bigfoot country."

The back seat of the car had become abnormally silent then, too. You could have heard a spring squeak, it was so quiet. It hadn't been. Beginning at nine o'clock that morning and continuing throughout the drive from the Pine Grove neighborhood in Monroe County, down State Road 446, out Chapel Hill Road and into the Guthrie Bottoms, across the State Road 37 four-lane, through Avoca and Springville, cross-country to Fayetteville and out to Silverville, it had been a pretty noisy backseat with Bigfoot talk. Some of it went like this.

"What are you going to do when we find Bigfoot?"

"I'm going to run!"

"I'm going to look in his eyes."

"I'm going to punch him."

"I'm going to see if he looks like the Abominable Snowman."

7

"He looks like Sasquatch."

"That's what Indians call Bigfoot. Sasquatch."

(Shrieks of laughter)

"Are you really going to take us to see Bigfoot?"

What else could have got me out of bed so early on a Sunday morning. What else could have kept me awake half the night praying that we would not find Bigfoot.

"Of course I'm going to take you to see him," I said aloud. "We'll go down to Silverville, take a look at him, and come right back home."

And to myself I added, "In a big hurry if we see him."

Home, I continued to myself, where I'll be safe and where I can fulfill all the promises I have been making to my unkept house and yard for the past few weeks.

"Let's go!"

It was like the sudden onset of pain. We had stopped at the Hawkins residence early that morning and zooom! Toot was in the back seat. Zooom! Tony had joined him. Zooom! Tracy was there beside them. Zooom! Lori . . .

Lori???

"She's our niece," I was informed. "She stayed overnight." Zooom! Nancy was in the front seat between us.

And lest we forgot our purpose for being alive that Sunday morning, Tracy had brought along an eight-chapter book titled, "The Abominable Snowman."

We could not have foreseen then that because of our ensuing frightening experience with Bigfoot that day we would be until five o'clock that afternoon finishing it.

Two, maybe three chapters into the abominable book, we arrived at Silverville. As our entire route

8

had been that morning, we found the community lifeless. Except for the churches. There were people at all the churches we passed, a sight that did little to soothe my burning conscience. Maybe there were no people. But what were all those cars doing in the parking lots? Try, try, and try as one might, there is no way to justify a Bigfoot hunt against the need to be in church on Sunday morning. Unless, of course, Bigfoot would be in church. But come to think of it, who'd want to be in church with Bigfoot? Or anyplace else, for that matter. So what were we doing out there?

We drove to the west end of Silverville and turned around. We'd seen Barney (he's better known as Barney than Bernard) Gallagher standing in his driveway on the way past, and decided to ask him some questions. He stood there looking at us as though he was puzzled at why the circus was out so early on a Sunday morning and stopped in his driveway. When we apprised him of what we were doing his answer was quick.

"Well, you're almost there," he said.

That's when the first awful quiet came from the back seat and from Nancy in between us.

If one of us had just thought to shout Booo! after Barney had waved a hand and said, "Take a sharp right there, go about a mile, and you'll be in Bigfoot country," the entire back seat would have zoomed all the way back to the Pine Grove community on a magic carpet of sheer will, with Nancy hanging on to its tassels.

No one did, of course, but one look into the back seat revealed those little noses twitching, sniffing for the smell of dead fish.

That's the Bigfoot stink, you know.

You smell dead fish and you've got Bigfoot within catching distance.

9

You will either catch him or he will catch you.

At least that's what we read in the newspaper one day. That is what elevated the interest of my little hunter companions.

Andy Keith, of near Silverville, had reported seeing Bigfoot and had told a newspaper reporter, "When I passed the area he (he being Bigfoot) was in there and it stunk like dead fish."

That's the reason why, as the car hiked around that sharp turn to the right, as Barney had pointed out, the only sound that came from the back seat was that of sniffing noses, fearing the tell-tale stink of dead fish.

Suddenly it seemed to fall on us with the suddenness of a thunder clap, nearly scaring us out of our wits. From the far corner of the front seat came the announcement:

"CHAPTER FOUR, THE ABOMINABLE SNOW-MAN"

The Bonannobble WHAT! WHERE?

"When are we going home!" squeaked Lori.

"We are not going home," I announced very bravely. "At least not until we find Bigfoot. You wanted to find Bigfoot. We're going to find Bigfoot. Look, there are two fellows playing pass with a football in front of that house. Let's stop."

That's how we had found Junior Tharpe. He leaned toward the car window. "You're in Martin County now," he advised.

Then in answer to another question he said, "Sure I saw Bigfoot. Several times."

Junior — his full name was William Henry Tharpe and he was twenty-one years old — said, "He was close." Then waving a hand in our direction he added, "From here to you."

At that disclosure the little Bigfoot hunters in the

back seat pushed themselves as far into the uphol-
stery as they could. Bigfoot having been so near to
Junior Tharpe as "From here to you," was simply too
close.

"When are we going home," Lori squeaked again.

"That was a few years ago," Junior continued.
There was an audible sigh of relief from the back seat.
"It was in the morning. But I didn't notice any stink
of dead fish."

But Junior, the newspaper said . . .

"No stink," repeated Junior. "But I'll tell you this
much. Whatever he is, he is here."

Then Junior said something that very nearly ended
the Sunday morning hunt for the creature known as
Bigfoot. As I remember it, this is what he said:

"One night when my sister, Jackie, went out to the
car to get some cigarettes he grabbed her."

"Let's go home," Lori squeaked twice as loudly as
she had done the two previous times.

No one, not a single, solitary Bigfoot hunter was
heard to say, "No, I don't want to go home."

Not a single, solitary Bigfoot hunter said "Hush" to
Lori. They were too brave.

So brave they were shaking all over.

So brave that if the car had turned around on its
own and raced back to Pine Grove they wouldn't have
raised a finger to stop it.

Against their better judgment we continued the
hunt.

When we dared, we parked the car and hunted
Bigfoot on his own terms — on foot around the edges
of a big cornfield.

We had decided by majority vote that there was no
need to hunt the surrounding dense woods and hills.

We'd already done that from the windows of the
moving car. As we hunted we walked fearlessly in a

tight bunch; we cut a cattail; we picked up a walnut. The wind blew through the tall corn stalks with a disturbing rustling, moaning sound.

"Let's go back to the car," squeaked Lori from the center of the group.

When the stink of dead fish became unbearable, which it soon did, we ran back to the car and closed the windows and locked the doors just as the voice from the far corner of the front seat boomed again: "CHAPTER FIVE . . ."

The Bananable Shasquamacallit was breathing down our collars. And STI-I-I-INK!

It was terrible!

Dead fish!

We fled.

Almost on its own the car turned in the direction of Pine Grove. During the ride back through Bigfoot country we listened to Chapter Six, Chapter Seven and Chapter Eight of the Abomb . . . Squash . . . Whatever.

Finally we were home safe and sound.

After the close call we had experienced, we were happy to be there.

ENCOUNTER AT THE SPRINGHOUSE

Was it a bird of ill omen that Julia saw above the springhouse that day miles away from her grand-daughter's deathbed, or was it in fact the child herself.

Ponder this:

In the days before electricity, when the telephone and the automobile were uncommon to the primitive hills and hollows of south central Indiana, there lived in the back country a woman purported to be possessed of strange powers.

Her name was Julia. It was said that she was able to cure certain childhood illnesses, and that mothers with babes in arms walked from miles around hoping to find in her a cure for their ailing children.

Those whose children reportedly were cured of certain illnesses by her looked upon Julia as a kind and benevolent woman, an angelic benefactress. Some of those who were fortunate enough to never have need of her strange powers, and those whose sick young she was unable to cure, whispered that Julia might be a witch. The latter was more than likely influenced by another strange power the woman had; the delicate, inelegant reception of omens, and por-tents of death. In that sense, the implication passed on to later times was that Julia was possessed of her powers through a compact with an evil spirit, or, as that spirit is better known, Satan.

In light of the woman's lifestyle, the claim appeared ludicrous. She was a kind, good woman to those in good health as well as to those in bad health, she was a loving mother and grandmother, as well as a good neighbor and friend.

So, then, was it a bird of ill omen that Julia saw at the springhouse that day so long ago? Was it her granddaughter?

13

Consider this: it is known that on that day one of her granddaughters, a child, lay mortally ill several miles from Julia's home. The good woman had exhausted her powers of healing in a futile attempt to save the child, and in deep sorrow had returned to her home to wait there for news of the little girl's death or her miraculous recovery.

It is also known that the kind woman so many called a witch had wept bitterly at her own helplessness while at the bedside of the sick child, and that her tears were still in abundance when, on the long walk back to her home, she had met friends and neighbors on the hilly footpath. It is known, too, that in the ensuing days, Julia often loudly bemoaned her inability to spend more time with the sick girl, and, travel being what it was in those days, that she was unable to visit her sick granddaughter as often as she would have liked.

After the encounter at the springhouse Julia returned home in a state of excitement. She related to her own family that while she was emerging from the springhouse she heard what she at first thought was a giant bird, flapping its wings. When she looked up, she told her family, she was shocked to see her sick granddaughter, "Flying overhead like an angel," she said.

The time was four o'clock in the afternoon.

On the following day a relative arrived at Julia's house by horse and buggy to inform the woman of the death the previous day of the sick child.

Later, after the funeral, the child's aggrieved mother told the following strange story.

Before the child died she had lapsed into a deep coma. But the unnatural sleep had lasted only minutes, for she had revived and said to her mother, "I went to Grandma's house for a few minutes."

Then she closed her eyes in death, the mother said. The hour was noted to be four o'clock in the afternoon, the exact time that Julia had her experience at the springhouse.

Was it a bird of ill omen, then, that Julia saw above the springhouse far away from where her little granddaughter lay dying? Or was it the child herself, bidding one last farewell to her anguished grandmother?

The encounter at the springhouse is only one of many strange incidents to happen in the hills and hollows of south central Indiana. It is also but one of such incidents to occur to Julia. Other messages were to come to her in her lifetime, and they too were orally recorded in the usual hand-me-down method of earlier times. One of these was an event referred to simply as "The water bucket and the tin cup."

It goes like this: Julia's attention was attracted one day to the water bucket sitting on a cabinet top in her kitchen. That was not unusual, for the bucket was always there. What was unusual was that the tin cup that always accompanied the water bucket on the cabinet was mysteriously flailing itself against the inside of the bucket, as though it were in the grasp of an unseen hand.

Next day, a visitor arrived at Julia's home by car, bearing the message informing Julia that a daughter of hers, living in another state, had died the previous day.

At the wake Julia asked her son-in-law if her daughter had spoken any last words. "Yes," he replied, "she had." They were strange words, but he recounted them to Julia anyway. "She said that she would like to have a drink from her mother's spring back home," he said.

The time of her daughter's passing coincided with the time the tin cup banged against the water bucket in Julia's home. The woman and her family were convinced that the incident was of supernatural origin.

***

Harbingers of death and evil are many, requiring only the ability to recognize them by sight and sound — such as the moon-less night howling of a dog, the moonlit-night hoot of an owl, or the nighttime appearance of fox fire.

Fox fire? It has been told that a husband and wife walking across a field to their home one night after church services saw a luminescent flickering of fox fire in their path. Frightened they turned their steps obliquely to avoid it, but the fox fire moved into their new path. They turned in the opposite direction, and there it was again, in front of them, ominously flickering its bluish-green light.

Shielding their eyes with their hands, they continued their terrified journey home, When they arrived there, they were met at the door by one of their own children. And in the eerie light provided by the fox fire, they saw that she was holding their infant daughter in her arms— dead.

SURPRISE

The road sign was tempting. After all, how often does a fellow find a town named Surprise? And this one, according to the green and white information sign, was only a half mile from the highway, on a narrow blacktop. So I turned south and began watching for it. I found an abandoned, ivy-covered, brick school building, a store, and about a dozen houses, but surprise, surprise, there was no town.

No town as such, anyway. It was quiet, like small communities traditionally are quiet. Jack Reichenbacker was in his backyard, in front of an open garage, working on a mower. Three straight-back chairs were arranged in a semi-circle in the garage, just back from the open door enough to be out of the sun.

Jack was gracious. No, he didn't know anything about the town, he said. And he laughed a good, healthy, happy laugh.

"Surprise? Well, I'll tell you. This place'll surprise me if it ever makes a town," he managed to say. "No, I don't know who knows anything about it. But I'll get Shirley out here. Maybe she knows someone."

Jack rapped four times on the side of the house with a screwdriver handle. The back door of the white frame opened and a smiling lady leaned out. She didn't know anyone who could tell me anything about the town, she informed me happily. "But," she added, "it is good to get outside in the hot sun; the air conditioner inside is awful cold."

The day wasn't planned in this manner. I had started out for Brown County. To make the trip interesting, I planned to go by way of State Road 135, past Houston, Story, and Stone Head. Whatever the season, that always is an enjoyable trip. If it is begun by

17

taking State Road 58 east, instead of US 50, it becomes a complete joy of Hoosier scenery.

It was no trouble. I had done it before, numerous times. State Road 58 winds through Zelma (the natives call it "Zelmy"), and Kurtz, and eventually it reaches State Road 135 south of Freetown. It was that little burg that first tempted me. Not that I had not ever seen it. I had. I'd also taken a few meals at Reva's restaurant there.

At a secondhand store in Freetown I once bought a long, wooden table. One of the long edges of that thing, I remember, was scarred by burning cigarette butts, left there by some worker or workers too busy to smoke. It obviously was a commercial table of some kind; it reminded me of the tables I used to see in dry goods stores, heaped with fabrics or shirts and overalls. It was tall, had a drawer in the middle, and one end of its flat surface had many knife cuts in it. Don't misunderstand, it was not a piece of junk. On the contrary, after I had refinished it everyone who saw it wanted it.

Freetown, I rediscovered, was still the same exciting place. Men and boys sat on benches in front of one of the stores and watched the traffic pass by. Highjacked cars with roaring pipes, and riding a bicycle no-hands on the highway were sport. State Road 58 twisted through there, and if a motorist followed it the road eventually ran into State Road 258.

It was on State Road 258 that "the good egg people" (Rose Acre Farms, Inc.) were located. Is there anyone who has never eaten a Rose Acre Farms jumbo egg (usually filled with two golden yolks)? I didn't know they were situated there. A huge flag flew from the pole in front of the place, yards and yards of waving stars and stripes. It was beautiful and thrilling to see it up there; made the hairs on my forearms tingle so I thought they stood straight up.

Rose Acre Farms, Inc., came as a sort of surprise because it was beyond the Surprise turn-off. I had driven too far. But, had I not made that mistake I would never have seen that grand flag. It was no trouble to turn and retrace my steps. And in due time I found Jack, and he had rapped with the handle of a screwdriver for Shirley.

In time, too, I found Millicent (Millie) Eudy. Millie was not a native (I didn't think there were any natives of Surprise anymore), but she'd lived in the little place since the 1940's. She was there in 1963 when a tornado ripped into the Christian Church and flattened it. A new church was built and it was dedicated the following year.

That same twister tore the front room off Bruce Reedy's place, and injured him enough so that he required hospital treatment. And the thing broke all the windows and tore the porch off the home of George, Edna and Mary Findley, Millie's brother and two sisters. It also knocked apart a concrete block building.

It was suppertime on Friday, April 19, when it charged down out of the spring sky with its long, black tail whipping crazily.

Millie stood in her house and watched as trees nearby were uprooted like so many small plants. She watched as it continued its twisting destruction.

There was no warning. The twister had descended in shocking surprise on the little hamlet of Surprise.

Oscar Allman was generally referred to as the "mayor" of Surprise. When he died about ten years earlier the honorary cloak of office was assigned, however kindly or unkindly, to Millie.

"But," she pointed out, "that is just a title, there is no mayor — no nothing — of Surprise."

Although she had visited Surprise when she was a

*After seventy-seven years the abandoned school building at
Surprise, Ind., is overgrown with wildlife. A tree grows in front
of what used to be the main entrance.*

child, and had lived there many years, Millie was not aware of the origin of its name. She and others to whom I directed that question associated it somehow with the Milwaukee Railroad, whose unused and mussed bed still cut through the place. It seems that someone stuck his head out of a train window at what once was no more than a whistle-stop and called out, "We're here! Surprise!"

It must have been quite a place in the early 1920's. Under the green ivy on the front of the abandoned school I made out the date, "A.D. 1922."

In Easyville, back the way I'd travelled on State Road 258, Carlin Allman told me he'd gone to school there in Surprise, and that there were four large rooms in the building, but no toilets. He said that there were a lot of kids who used to go to school there. At this time some of the kids went to Courtland, and the older ones went to Seymour.

The building was privately owned, and had been for years, Millie said. She also said that its demolition had been in the talking stage for years.

Those things usually are. And, after all the talk, when they do happen, they come as a surprise. You've heard people say as much.

And speaking of surprises, people who've never heard of Surprise are usually surprised to hear residents say, "I'm from Surprise."

The response is generally, "Oh, what a surprise! I never knew there was a place by the name of Surprise."

I never did reach Houston, Story, and Stone Head that day. I didn't get to any part of Brown County. I got tempted by a road sign that read "Surprise."

PAUL NORRIS

Time was when a man reached the Biblical promise of three-score and ten he was considered to be in the precarious position of standing with one foot in the grave and the other on a banana peel.

That is not necessarily true.

When that age became the topic of a male gathering one day, an amusing anecdote about two over seventy-year-olds was recounted to illustrate that fact.

Supported by their canes, the two were out for a stroll. They were shuffling along a sidewalk when an attractive, shapely young lady came slithering and quivering from the opposite direction.

Catching his breath with a sudden gasping sound, one of the oldsters stopped in his tracks, leaned heavily on his cane, and ogled her longingly and lasciviously. After she passed he turned to lust after her some more.

Curious, his companion asked him what he was doing. Still leaning on his cane the oldster released a long, mournful sigh and replied, "I'm thinking how nice it would be to be seventy again."

During the continued three-score and ten discussion, I was reminded of a respectable family man who lived in Tulip, about a half dozen miles from Persimmon Ridge where I met him one day. His name was Paul Norris and he lived in the tiny Greene County hamlet with his wife, Laura, whom he lovingly called "Laurie."

Mr. Norris was mixing mortar with a hoe when I interrupted him. It was a beautiful sunny day, but hot. Ask anyone who has ever mixed mortar with a hoe, and he or she will tell you that hot weather or cold, it is back-breaking work. Mr. Norris wasn't just mixing mortar, he was mixing it to use in a concrete block wall he himself was laying up.

An estimated three hundred and fifty eight-inch

blocks were required to do the job and he planned to lift, carry and set each and every one.

At the time, Mr. Norris was already a year past his allotted three-score and ten. I was incredulous, for I was at an age when I thought three-score and ten was the end of the road.

Part of the wall Mr. Norris was building was already in place, and the mortar joints were neat and the course heights right on the money. It took but a glance to see that he was expert in what he was doing and not just an old man doddering around.

"Took me just about a day to lay those blocks," he smiled at my obvious surprise that at his age he should be doing that kind of manual labor. "Mixed my own mortar, carried the blocks myself, did it all myself."

Unimpressed by the compliments that poured from me, he said, "Not long ago I laid up a thousand blocks in just about two days."

Slight of build, about five-feet-seven, maybe a hundred and forty-five pounds, he laughed off my concern that he should be working so hard.

"Oh," he chortled, "I just do enough to make my sixteen-eighty."

A Social Security recipient, he was allowed to earn one thousand six hundred and eighty dollars over and above his annual retirement benefit. He held up a partially clenched left hand and smiled proudly, "And I do it all with this."

Mr. Norris then pulled back the sleeve of his green work shirt and exposed a deformed wrist.

"Got it caught in a stationary drill that tore it off," he explained. "Had on a gauntlet glove. Boy! That thing caught in the drill and it spun me around, knocked my teeth out and tore my hand off at the wrist, right here," he pointed with his right forefinger.

23

He stopped the drill by knocking a belt off a pulley, an act that probably saved his life, he said. Seeking help, he approached a co-worker who promptly fainted at the sight of the injury. Another co-worker came to his aid and transported him by automobile to the office of a Bloomfield physician.

"Old Doc Turner," Mr. Norris identified him. "He took one look and he gave me a drink and shot me in the arm and said, 'Get in my car.' And he took me to the hospital in Linton.

"Whatever that drink was, I don't know, but it made me meaner than hell," he continued. "Oh, I was mean. When we got to the hospital, they brought a cot to carry me on, and I told them I wasn't going to get on it, that I felt good enough to walk three miles."

Since it sounded like something I thought I should have had in my own medicine cabinet in case of emergency, I hoped to learn from Mr. Norris the ingredients of that drink.

"I don't know what that was," he said. "Hell, by that time I was in such a shape I'd have drunk anything and not known what it was."

He was taken to surgery where he got rammy again.

"I felt someone take hold of my other arm," he said, "and I asked old Doc who it was, and he said it was the prettiest nurse they had in the whole hospital. And I settled down.

"But you know," he added, "after they were done with me and I came around, that nurse came in to tell me it was her that was holding my arm. And she was the oldest one in the hospital."

Check in the back of this book for a list of titles of all Larry Incollingo's books and how you may obtain an autographed copy for yourself or a personalized copy for a friend or loved one.

TO MAKE A RAINBOW

It was Marie Dixon Ingle's birthday and in a noon-time salute to her achievement of another milestone, and to her continued good health, family and friends had gathered in the Tunnelton Senior Citizen Center to celebrate.

For the occasion, volunteer cooks Virginia Bennett and Izella Bush had prepared a savory country luncheon of meatloaf, baked beans, mashed potatoes, green beans, fresh-baked yeast rolls, other goodies, and, of course, a decorated cake.

While waiting to preside over the bounty, Marie took some time to tell me what it was like to reach a plateau just shy by a dozen years of the century mark. While she was at it she agreed to divulge her secret to longevity.

"It has its good points and it has its bad points," she said of piling up the years. "But," she added, "life has all been good enough that I'm going to play it cool from here, and hope to go on with it."

She expressed a single fear and a singular hope.

"I don't ever want to go to a nursing home," she said. "That does not appeal to me, and it's so hard on the family. When the time comes, I would like to do the George Burns act — just let the old heart quit ticking."

But for the benefit of those who would emulate her and make it through many years of living, she articulated her secret for a long life with these words of caution:

"First of all, don't ever let people know the shape you're in, or they might give you medication that will kill you."

Flushed with apparent good health, blue eyes sparkling behind spectacles that reflected the daylight, Marie laughed cheerily.

"You hear something like that every once in a while, you know. Someone will say about a person, 'He was feeling bad, so they gave him some medication. And it killed him.'

"Not me," she said firmly. "I'm not telling anyone if I feel bad. And you better not."

Fifty years ago she dared go to the blood bank as a potential donor. When they saw her, volunteer workers there frowned.

"Did you come to give or to get," she was asked.

"I never went back," Marie smiled at the memory. "I've always been puny, but healthy. I went to an old doctor once and he diagnosed me as having high blood pressure and anemia. 'Cut down on fats and salt,' he said, 'and never get over a hundred and forty pounds.'

"I just reached that weight, right now, after all these years. And I'm still doctoring for high blood pressure. So if you want to live a long life just don't get too healthy. Know what is wrong with you so you can take care of yourself."

The same old doctor recommended she drink a glass of wine a day to build up her blood.

"I never smoked or drank, except for that wine," she said. "I quit after the first bottle. That must have got my blood built up. At least it must have got me straightened out, for I sure didn't complain anymore."

Marie spent most of her long life in Tunnelton. A contemporary of the late school teacher Madge Crane, she graduated from Tunnelton High School in 1926. For many years after Madge had lost her eyesight, Marie picked up her mail at the post office, took it to Madge's house, and read it to her. Widowed twice, Marie had one daughter, Jo Jones, who used to write Tunnelton and Bono news for the Mitchell Tribune.

Marie spent several years as bookkeeper at Jenkins Electric, in Bedford. She lived across the street from the Tunnelton United Methodist Church and was the keeper of its keys and the keys to the church annex which also served as the Senior Center. She attended services at the church "every time the door opens," she said, and took her weekday lunches with other seniors at the annex.

"A long life doesn't necessarily add up to an easy life," Marie warned. "But it takes a little rain and a little sunshine to make a rainbow. And rainbows are awfully pretty. I have had lots of help from people here. That's the way this little town is; our community is our family, our neighbors are close and helpful. We entertain angels unaware."

A product of one-room school learning, Marie praised the wisdom of an era when poetry was a substantial part of school study and had to be read and memorized.

"Nowadays they don't do that in schools," she said. "They argue about teaching the Bible. We had God in our school through poetry. There's the way to get God into schools now. What so many poets have written reflects the Divine nature of God. 'The Song of Hiawatha,' is an example. But schools don't do that anymore, and people don't know. They have kids sitting around pecking on computers, and folks wonder why Johnny can't read."

Marie believed that a clear conscience is of utmost importance to health and longevity, and she pointed out the way to one in this manner:

"Everyone," she said, "makes mistakes. What so many people don't realize is that you can't go back and correct them. You've got to look up, look ahead, and keep going. You can't repeat your life. You've just got to shape up and do better."

And finally, she gave this familiar bit of advice: "Be nice to people. Do unto them as you'd have them do unto you."

KETCHAM

"Most of the time," Ralph Ketcham recalled living in Ketcham and attending Smithville High School, three miles distant, "we rode a horse, or in a buggy."

Ketcham found its beginnings shortly after the Indian wars, when the federal government deeded some two square miles of acreage south of Bloomington to Indian fighter Colonel John Ketcham.

The colonel was Ralph's great grandfather, and he established and operated there, until it burned to the ground early in this century, the four-story Ketcham Flour Mill. He lived nearby in a two-story log home, which in recent years was dismantled and moved away from that site.

Colonel Ketcham also granted a right of way across his land to the old Monon Railroad, with the proviso that the railroad company construct a depot at that point.

"They did that," Ralph said of the construction of the depot, "but the trains didn't stop there. Not until they put on the locals. But they never did keep an agent there."

Ralph spent the first thirty-eight years of his life in Ketcham, about two hundred yards across a pasture from the site of the old depot.

He recalled that two locals, one northbound and the other southbound (No. 9 and No. 10) passed there each day. Faster passenger trains included dining and sleeping cars.

"Sometime about 1900-10 or -12," Ralph reviewed some of his recollections of early times at Ketcham, "Indiana allowed the sale of liquor. But any county could vote to stay dry, and Monroe was for some time.

"Dining cars on the fast passenger trains could serve liquor in dry counties, as long as they were mov-

28

ing. I was a young boy then, but I remember hearing of people in Bloomington who would like a drink once in a while getting on a train at four in the afternoon and having a fine meal served with drinks on the diner.

"They would party until they met a northbound train down in southern Indiana and arrive back in Bloomington at midnight. Of course, there was a diner on that train, too, and those who wanted could

Railroad Station At Ketcham

party all the way back home."

As a boy Ralph attended the old Mitchell School, about a mile from Ketcham.

"It was probably named after Sam Mitchell, Dr. George Mitchell's father," Ralph opined. And he recalled that Dr. Mitchell began his practice at Quincy, "the first year I went to high school at Smithville."

Riding there on a horse, or in a buggy until his graduation fifty-nine years ago, Ralph traveled what was then "a pike road" named the Dixie Highway. There were seven graduates in the class of 1919. Ralph named them: Clifford Botkins, Jessie Deckard Adams, Ell Deckard Botkins, Marion Todd, Elizabeth Franz, Chester Wooten and, of course, Ralph himself.

"Three teachers were the most I ever did have in high school," Ralph recalled those days at Smithville High. "And they were all taken away, by the way, the next to the last year I was there."

The teachers were Frank Lindsey, Richard Cordell and John Adams, who also was the basketball coach.

"There were only nine boys in the whole school," Ralph said. "Just about enough for a basketball team. We had some good ones, too. But we could never win over Bloomington. There were so many more boys there, and so much bigger."

Ralph stood six-feet and played center and guard.

"I was a real tall boy in those days," he said with a wry smile.

His teammates included Ollie Stewart, Earl Chambers, Horace Chambers, Ernest Judah, Russell Litz and Gilbert Butcher.

"I remember some of the Bloomington players were Judge Donald Rogers, John Crane, Bob Markinson and Wyatt May," he said.

Back to Ketcham, where he was reared, Ralph rarely missed an opportunity to stop and watch passing trains pulled by the huff-puffing steam locomotives.

"I did like to see those old trains," he said. "Sometimes they'd kill stock that got on the right of way. And my mother's turkeys. We got paid for stock, but never for turkeys."

Two trains were involved in an accident in the

Ketcham pasture one day. One of the trains was standing at the time. The engineer of the second put it into emergency stop, but not quite soon enough.

Ralph recalled that the engine crew of the standing train abandoned it when they saw the other train approaching. There was much damage, but there were no injuries. When the fireman of the standing train returned to his damaged engine he indicated a fence he climbed on his return. "I didn't know that fence was there 'til I came back," Ralph quoted him.

Ralph, who was now seventy-eight, lived at 286 North Main Street, in Spencer, with his wife, Pearl Trisler Ketcham, who graduated from Smithville High in 1918, in what then was considered to be a large class – ten graduates.

He was a retired farmer, and more recently he retired from a retail farm implement sales in Spencer.

He guessed he was about fifteen when the old Ketcham depot was razed. The building was being carried away piecemeal by vandals, and by area residents who used the lumber for kindling. The Monon replaced it with an old box car, and that was used as the Ketcham depot until it too was removed.

"Sometimes, around 1910, I'd go across our field and flag No. 10 about 7:30 in the morning and board the train for Bloomington," Ralph said. "As a kid I went for half-fare; a nickel. In Bloomington I'd go to the southwest corner of the square to Dr. Luzzader's office over the First National Bank and spend the day riding in his beautiful Marion Roadster, making house calls.

"I remember one time he and another man made a survey of the number of autos in Bloomington. They were surprised to learn that there were 110 in the town.

"Dr. Luzzader was our family doctor. I would eat

my noon and evening meals with them and then catch No. 9, pay my fare, and get home about 7:30 p.m., after a wonderful day in Bloomington," Ralph said.

When World War One began, "America," Ralph continued, "went into high production and farm prices began to get higher.

"In 1916 my father sold a pair of mules for $350.00 and bought a Ford touring car for $360.00.

"Wages were going up and everybody enjoyed prosperity and nearly everyone bought a car of some kind. That," he said, "was the beginning of the end of the 'Golden Age of Passenger Trains' in America."

The twisty-turny railroad in and around Ketcham was popularly known as the "Punkinvine." And if you would care to check, Ralph said, "You'll find that in the eight miles between Clear Creek and Harrodsburg, the Punkinvine crosses the creek thirteen times."

Having "grown up" almost on the punkinvine, Ralph said he came to love the trains that ran over its rails, and the men who operated them.

"I knew several engine men and train men. I saw many wrecks near our home, and actually delivered some messages taken over our party line to the train crews. But," he concluded, "all that is another story."

The two-story white house in which he was born and reared still stands at Ketcham. Should you pass there sometime stop and listen for the huff-puffing of the old steam locomotives on the Punkinvine.

PERRY

In the fire log of the Perry Township Volunteer Fire Department in Monroe County there is the following entry:

"May 11, 1970. 2 p.m.

"Charles Oakes brought dog to the fire station. Breed, Dalmatian. Age, ten weeks. Born February 25th, 1970. Name: 'Perry the First'."

Like big city fire departments, Perry Township Volunteer Fire Department was going to have its own Dalmatian dog riding the fire apparatus.

But it didn't quite work out that way.

"He keeps throwing up in our hip pockets," said paid driver Bill Hobbs.

Bill said he spoke to a veterinarian about Perry's problem.

"The vet said he could give us some pills for him," Bill noted, "but we'd have to give him one an hour before a fire run."

It all sounded like a joke.

"No joke," said Charles (Chuck) Oakes, chief of the thirty-man volunteer department. "It's the truth. We were on our way to a fire one day and Perry was chained between me and the driver. All of a sudden I got this warm, wet feeling in my hip pocket."

Chuck, and John Cassidy, made up one twelve-hour shift of paid drivers while Bill, and Rex Walters, made up the other shift. They'd been working with Perry, but the handsome black and white thirty-five pound dalmation had yet to completely overcome his motion sickness.

"Bill's been working with him," said Chuck. "He'll jump up into the cab when we go out on a run, but we put him out and make him stay here on station. He minds well. Bill will have him so he can ride one of these days."

33

Bill talked to Perry to keep him from getting sick while riding. The talking worked on the way to a fire at the county dump one day. Perry didn't throw up. However, the smoke and the stench of that fire undid all the talking Bill was capable of, and Perry got sick on the way back. And he threw up again.

As dogs go, Perry the First was not only handsome, he was beautiful. At little more than seven months, he'd grown to be a fairly good-sized animal, and he was expected to have a lot of growing ahead of him. He was big enough at seven months, however, that he was not allowed to sleep on the couch at headquarters anymore. His bed was in the front seat of a brush fire truck.

Despite his size, Perry thought he was still a puppy. After being babied by thirty men for most of his life, he believed he was still a lap dog. Alas, it just didn't work out that way anymore. There was not enough lap in the whole fire department membership to accommodate him.

He nevertheless was still a loved possession around headquarters. Although he was fed twice a day, once more than the average pet dog, the guys brought him additional rations in the form of steak and other meat scraps from home.

"That," mused Chuck one day, "could be part of the reason why he gets sick."

Perry was not only a mascot to the Perry Township Volunteer Fire Department, he was a member.

"You'd better believe it," said Chuck.

Although he had not yet learned to make a hydrant connection fireman style, or a hose-coupling, he did leave his paw prints in a freshly poured concrete sidewalk at the rear of the township building; an accidental incident that required a refinishing of the new surface. One day he climbed up to the table in the dining area and ate John Cassidy's freshly prepared TV dinner. And for some time he escaped identification as the thief who was stealing township trustee secretary Sue Dixon's luncheon sandwiches from her office.

Perry the First also had learned to chase bugs and spiders and anything else that crawled.

"He likes to play with them," said Chuck. "And he likes a lot of people. When we have training programs he's right in the middle of things until we tell him to go off and lie down someplace. He'll do as we tell him and just lie there and watch every move we make."

To one side of the concrete step that led from the fire truck bays to the crew's living and lounging quarters, there is inscribed in the concrete these words:

"Perry the First," along with Perry's paw print. Perry had all the required shots to make him a safe pet. And pet he was.

"All the kids in the neighborhood come to see him," said Chuck. "They like him, and Perry likes them."

"Isn't Perry an odd name for a dog," I asked.

"We couldn't very well call him 'Van Buren', (another Monroe County township volunteer fire company)" said John Cassidy.

"No," added Chuck. "We couldn't call him 'Bloomington' either (still another such county fire company)."

Had he remained a pup, Perry might still be lounging around the fire station. But Perry's healthy growth and maturity, accompanied by the realization that he was a macho male, led to his demise.

"He took to tom-cattin' around," said a fireman.

Tom-CATTIN'?

What an epitaph for poor Perry.

Well, I suppose the truth is the truth. Perry's amorous wanderings took him to Walnut Street Pike one day and, intent as he was on the pleasures the day might afford, he unknowingly trotted into the path of an automobile.

Females and cars have undone many a male's ambition, and Perry was to be no exception. He was hospitalized for about a week. The vet exhausted every technique trying to keep him alive, and the fellows at the fire station wished real hard that their dog would get well. Some of them might even have prayed for their pet.

But Perry's condition did not improve. As a matter of fact, he got about as worse as he could get. And Charlie Oakes and Randy Sciscoe, a relief driver, buried him under crossed fence posts at the rear of the fire station on the Perry Township Building lot.

"We gave him a decent burial, with all the honors," Randy said.

They hung Perry's collar on the station bulletin board and it remained there for the duration of a decently lengthy mourning period, and then it was taken down and put away.

Perry was not forgotten, however. A photograph of the black and white dog was tacked to the bulletin board for all to see, for all to remember. It was a head shot, and a good likeness of Perry.

The volunteers, for some time after his death, received other reminders of their pet. A constant one was that fire runs were throw-up-free, and volunteers no longer found it necessary to wash out their hip pockets and the cabs of their fire trucks afterwards.

THE PERANDA

Logan Hatfield was probably one of the best carpenters to ever drive a nail in the rural community of Owensburg. He could build almost anything, and his charges were considered reasonable. He also was one of the most sought after preachers. But it wasn't for preaching that sent Aunt Ell looking for Logan. It was for his primary talent — carpentering. She wanted him to build a peranda for her, the very name of which aroused the curiosity of almost everyone in town.

Long before Logan built her peranda Aunt Ell's name was never mentioned without the appendage, "She's a Civil War widow." And it was not rare that people should add, "She gets a Civil War pension." It piqued the interest of some folks and galled some others that she would never disclose just how large or small a pension she received. Some guessed fifty dollars a month, others, sixty dollars. They all agreed, however, that either of those amounts was a lot of money in those days.

When the news got around that Aunt Ell was going to have a peranda added to her house, curiosity ran rampant. For one thing, people had never heard of one. When she let it be known that it was pension money scrupulously put aside each month that would finance the cost of it and pay Logan his wages for building it, they were further agog with wonder and expectancy.

Logan hadn't much more than got started on the project when townspeople suffered a major let-down. They discovered Aunt Ell's much talked about peranda was nothing more than a porch. And folks learned something else. Although Aunt Ell had often spoken of her desire for a peranda, the woman, in all her

37

years, had never learned to properly pronounce v-e-r-a-n-d-a with a V.

Life's full of such shocking disappointments. But folks rallied from that blow and to their everlasting credit always kindly referred to the new porch as "Aunt Ell's Peranda." It was a handsome thing. Enclosed with red brick rails, red brick pilasters rose high from its corners and from each side of its entrance. From the top of the limestone coping on the pilasters, tapered wooden columns rose to support the shingled hip roof. It was said that it was the most handsome peranda Logan had ever built.

When it was learned that the total cost of the peranda was five hundred dollars, people were aghast. They didn't just say "Five hundred dollars?" They gasped, "FIVE HUNDRED DOLLARS?!!!!" An amount which in Owensburg in those days was about equal to all the money in the world. And they wondered if the old widow's Civil War pension wasn't more than they had suspected.

There was more. Aunt Ell directed Luke Corbin to paint the tapered columns white. On the face of each one of them she had him paint a potted red geranium. And folks agreed that it was not only the most handsome peranda in town, it also was the prettiest.

When Aunt Ell died in 1936, her peranda and house to which it was attached paid off her last worldly obligations. For a number of years it was rented to various families. What would have been pleasing to Aunt Ell, though, was that in the late 1940s the occupants of her house began giving it meticulous care. And for the next eighteen years it was a lovely place. Painted white with green trim, flowers overflowing the planters atop the brick rails of the peranda, and evergreens thriving on either side of the entrance, it really caught the eye of every passerby.

More pleasing to Aunt Ell, had she been able to see them, would have been the great number of people who came to gather in clusters under the protective roof of her peranda where they gawked and jabbered as folks normally do at funerals. For during those eighteen years Aunt Ell's beloved peranda was the attractive entrance to a funeral home.

When I pass through Owensburg I am aware that the house and peranda are now rotating somewhere in oblivion, out of sight and mind of every living soul except some roving newspaper reporter. While I dare feel Logan Hatfield couldn't care less, I can't help but wonder if any of this could still possibly matter to Aunt Ell, wherever she may be.

NELLARAY
ONE FOR THE RECORD BOOK

If you have ever felt a yearning for peace, had a longing to get away from everyone and everything, if you'd like to thrill again to a beautiful sunset, bathe undisturbed in moonglow, and you also think such thoughts are silly for someone your age, come and meet Nellaray Borton Holt.

Nellaray was probably just as old as you. Maybe older. She had retired more than fifteen years before I met her. She was probably shorter than you, too, about four-feet-ten. She had lovely blue eyes, a pesky hip that was held together with four pins, she wore glasses, full dentures and was in need of a hearing aid.

Moreover, a young woman whom she had mothered for years, and whose lifestyle Nellaray could no longer support, told her to go to hell. Finally, her own mother so hated the name Nellaray she would never speak it.

Unless you take into account that Nellaray claimed that her name was listed in the Guinness Book of World Records, she was probably not that different from you, with maybe one exception. Long before that achievement she had to tear herself from the grasp of old rocking chair. Just like you'll have to do if you want the fun out of life that she had discovered.

Nellaray was a tree expert. That's right. And one of the many benefits she derived from what she did was traveling and meeting people.

In her own words, "I don't think there's a state I haven't been in, I've met all kinds of wonderful people, and everybody is so nice to me," she said.

She did her traveling in one of those Toyota mini-motorhomes you wonder what the insides are like when you see one of them pass.

"I call mine 'The Guppy.'" she nodded toward the little thing parked outside the English post office. "It's fifteen feet long, has a bed — a dinette that makes a bed — sink, refrigerator, stove, heater, plenty of storage space, and a portable bathroom. You can stick it up on a shelf when it's not needed. I seldom use it because I'm usually at a court house someplace anyway," she said. She was in English to visit the Crawford County Courthouse.

She used to live in Yakima, Washington. Then Mesquite, Nevada. Holtville, California. At this time she lived a little closer to English — Quartzsite, Arizona. But, because of her line of work, home was a moveable joy, and nights there were spent where she parked it; usually in a church parking lot, by a police station, or near a courthouse.

Nellaray's particular tree expertise took her to courthouses a lot. She was a family-tree expert. That's right. And that's what got her into the Guinness Book of World Records. At the time of our meeting she had completed three hundred and seven books on families throughout the USA. The largest one, the one that got her into the record book, was a family tree measuring eighteen feet by fifteen feet. It contained six thousand eight hundred and twenty names of relatives extending back to 1562, and took sixteen years to complete. To get a picture of it, she had to unroll it out of a second floor window.

People paid her to do their trees. Usually people who were too busy to do it themselves, and who had enough money to pay her to do it for them; like doctors. Doing family trees was how she got into the "The Guppy," too. Some doctor clients got together and bought it for her. They wanted her to be comfortable, and self-sufficient. Besides "The Guppy" painted on it, she has painted her name on it, too, "Nellaray," the name her mother hated.

"My father named me after his grandfather," she explained its origin. "And my mother hated the name Nellaray so much she refused to ever say it. I'm surprised she didn't flatten me with a frying pan when I was a baby."

Nellaray was an ex-librarian. She had six children of her own. Several others moved in on her. And it was one of the latter who one day suggested Nellaray go to that awful place.

"None of my own children ever talked to me like that," she gritted at the memory. "I couldn't handle it. My old heart was just a-rocking like this," she moved her fists up and down over her chest. "I wanted to bust her in the mouth, but I couldn't get to her," she said.

Nellaray was doing a family tree that took her to a rural cemetery on a ridge in New York when the ground gave way under her. Mudslide! Broken hip. Hospital. Four pins to put it back together. One of the hazards of tree experting, she smiled.

"But it's exciting," she said. "People think because they're retired they have to sit in a rocking chair. I don't believe in that. I tell the good Lord, 'I still have things I want to do,' and I keep going.

"I yearned for peace, to get away from everyone, to watch the moon rise, see the sun come up. This gives me that opportunity, and the opportunity to get away from my five great grandchildren," she said.

IVAN, THE GREATEST

If you've tried everything else and still can't quit cigarettes, you might want to try Ivan Lindsey's cure. He says that given a chance it'll work, and it won't cost an arm and a leg as does a pack of cigarettes. Not even a single red cent.

It's this way: While seated at a table, place a pack of smokes in front of you along with a lighter. Just sit there patiently and wait. And if God wants you to smoke, Ivan says, "He'll take a cigarette out of the pack, put it in your mouth, and strike the lighter for you."

Don't like that method? He has this other one he says worked like a charm for him.

"I put a small New Testament in my shirt pocket where I always carried my cigarettes," he said. "Each time I reached for a cigarette I touched that Testament, and each time I touched it I took it out of my shirt pocket and read something from it. In four days I not only didn't want another cigarette, I couldn't stand to be around cigarette smoke."

Ivan was not in the business of giving out smoking cures. He was just a modern Good Samaritan in the business of helping people. Mostly American veterans, whom he helped in any way that he could, including bringing them pleasure. But feeling the way he did about smoking, he offered, as friendly advice to the otherwise hopelessly addicted, these means to quit.

"I almost died a couple of times," he said of ridding himself of the habit of inhaling cancer sticks, "and I'm not going to kill myself over something stupid, like smoking."

His brushes with death had nothing to do with cigarettes, nor with smoking or with tobacco of any kind.

43

The first one happened on his entry into the world.

"I was such a mess when I was born the doctor flipped me over on a bench and told my mother, 'This child is done for,' and turned away from me," he began recounting those precarious early minutes of life as told to him later. "I was one of eleven children of a farmer and his wife, and it might not have made a difference to that doctor if I lived or died. But the midwife who was there wouldn't give up on me. She began shaking me and breathing into my mouth and before long she had me breathing."

That experience, however scary, remains a distant second to the time he was given up for dead in the Korean War.

"I woke up in a refrigerated compartment, naked and freezing, with my dog tags in my mouth and a 'Dead On Arrival' tag tied to my left big toe," he remembered. "Now that was something. The dead were being carried down to the lowest level of a ship for transport back to the U.S. And there I was, supposed to be dead, when somebody said, 'Hey, this guy's breathing.'"

As happened with his first brush with death, he also learned of this more frightening experience second-hand.

"When I heard all this from my buddy I told him, 'Hey, don't tell me any more. You are scaring me to death,'" Ivan recalled.

Ivan was eighteen when he enlisted in the Army during the Korean War. He was sure he'd never see home again after he was assigned to an outfit popularly known as "The Bayonet Regiment." Three months later while he and his buddies were attempting to re-take Charlie Company's hill it seemed the end had come.

He remembers very little about that fight, but witnesses saw enough of what he did before he was wounded and left for dead that Ivan was awarded a medal for heroism and valor; for saving the life of another soldier. He wears the award along with a Purple Heart and other medals and the coveted Combat Infantryman's Badge on his Disabled American Veterans uniform.

"I don't remember any of that combat," he said in a rich baritone. "I'm no hero. The heroes are all dead." A friendly, medium-sized fellow who wore glasses, you probably saw him at fairs and festivals and in parades. He was conspicuous in a neatly pressed black uniform trimmed in gold braid, with colorful ribbons all over the chest of his Ike jacket and chaplain crosses on the shoulder boards.

A retired disabled Army staff sergeant, he was chaplain of the Disabled American Veterans, Bedford Chapter 2. An unheralded volunteer, he spent his time helping disabled American veterans in any way that he could. But he did not restrict his aid to them. A truly good Samaritan with limited income and resources, he made himself available to anyone and everyone for any and all the needs that were within his power to give.

"I'm just trying to do like my father and mother," he explained his innate interest in others. "I don't get much of a retirement, but each month I set aside money to help others. I take them to stores, to the doctor's office, to the veterans hospital and wherever they need to go. My father taught me that if you have to go out of your way to help someone, do it. That's what I'm doing."

His mother played the organ at church, and although she had eleven children, on Sunday morning after milking she'd harness the team and get all the kids ready to go to church. "We were taught Christian values on a daily basis at home, and every Sunday in church," Ivan said.

Whether you believe in those values or not, you have to believe in people like Ivan. He was asked once how he was able to make it safely back home from the war in Korea. His reply fit his teaching. "Because," he said, "a lot of people back home were on bended knees praying for me."

He remembered the Korean experience as "A downhill drag that became an uplift to God. I had a Christian upbringing, but I had never given my life to Christ," he continued. "After what happened to me in Korea it didn't take me long to get to Christ. That was in July. I celebrate that event every July, even more than my birthday."

"WE WERE HAPPY HERE"

Had Earl and Helen Miller been young, a team of mules couldn't have pulled them away from the Lick Creek bottoms of Owen County and the two-story home in which they'd spent the sixty-one years of their marriage when I met them.

They were not young, and despite the memories with which the old homestead abounded, Earl and Helen, on the eve of their final days there, were content to be leaving the one hundred eighty-six acre farm.

"I ain't going to miss the hard work," said Earl with a hint of a smile.

"I can't say that I'm happy about leaving," Helen observed. "I know all the people around here. But my husband said the place was getting to be too much for him, and I won't contrary him."

She smiled pleasantly then and said, "But I'll come back to ride past in the car, and maybe visit with the neighbors. He promised me that before I'd sign the papers."

The neighbors would have been about all that was left when she did return. Most of the material things that went into making their home, those things that fit into living together for more than a half century, would be gone, sold at auction.

She guided me to the three rooms upstairs and the three downstairs where she, her husband, and their three children had lived together for so long. All were virtually bare, the things of life that once filled them now filled boxes and baskets pushed together on their floors, waiting to be sold at auction.

Brimming boxes and baskets also lined the house walls outside on the continuing porch around three sides of the house. On a slope above several outbuildings, the implements with which Earl had tilled the land, and those with which he had harvested his many labors, lay like hired hands sleeping in neat, silent ranks, also awaiting the unfeeling call of the auctioneer.

"If I were young," Helen smiled somewhat wistfully, "I wouldn't go. I always liked living here. In the summer the porch was such a nice place to sit."

She remembered her children, and she laughed.

"I was always quite a bit of the kid," she said looking toward the slope, the outbuildings and land and the house as one. "I'd get out there and play with them. Like I was one of them."

She reflected on those pleasures for the briefest moment, then said, "I miss them a lot."

Earl and Helen were as much a part of the Lick Creek bottoms country as was anyone. Earl was brought to the very house they were leaving at age one, when his parents moved into it. Helen grew up in Antioch, a few miles away. She attended eight grades in a one-room school there, and Earl attended eight in the Precinct School not too distant from there.

Gran'paw Miller had set pine trees on either side of the walk that led from the roadside to the old house long before then. They were growing there in Earl's and Helen's childhood days, and during the days of their youth. They were still there; tall, their massive boles symbolic of the permanence people once brought to a land.

"I never thought about leaving," Helen said of the couple's decision to buy a home in the town of Worthington. "We were happy here. When Earl couldn't find a hired hand I used to go out and help him.

"I used to harrow, milk the cows, cut wood, cut corn, and do everything there was to do on a farm, just like a man would do. We never thought about being some-place else."

That possibility had occurred to them thirteen years before my visit with them, when Helen fell and broke her thigh. They recalled that day: Helen was alone and was going to call Hazel Summerlot on the telephone. She turned to sit in a chair and — she was unable to account for her bad aim — she missed it and sat heavily on the floor.

"I lay there for two hours, until Earl came in," she said. "Then he dragged me out on the porch. He brought the car up, and lifted me in and took me to the doctor. I was a bit sore," she remembered.

Earl didn't quite "drag" her.

"It was June 14, 1965," he remembered the incident. "It was on a Saturday, about four o'clock. She was nervy and had a lot of grit. She didn't complain. I got her into a chair then I dragged her out on the porch," he said.

"I had an awful time getting her into the car," he continued. "Just one person trying to do that, you know, it's a hard job. And I didn't want to hurt her."

Earl was seventy-two at that time, and he wasn't the youth he was back in June of 1917 when he carried Helen across the threshold of their house, the house they were preparing to leave. The incident left its mark on him.

"Just the two of us out here," he said shaking his head , "it makes you think a little, you know."

Their new home was comprised of five rooms, and it was near enough to downtown Worthington to place it within walking distance of all the couple's needs.

"I'm not going to worry about the winters there," Earl said looking forward to their move. "If this winter's going to be as bad as last winter, why then we'll all have it. It won't be just us out here."

The previous winter they were cut off from Coal City, two miles west, Freedom, six miles east, Patricksburg, eight miles north, and Worthington, eight miles south.

Continuing with the light mood, Earl looked out on the Lick Creek bottoms, Fiscus Cemetery, and the homes within sight of his vantage point in the front yard. He swung an arm like a wand.

"I've hunted all over there," he said. "Lots of coon hunters have too. But I'm going to miss the squirrel hunting most of all. But," he adjusted his glasses, "I can't see to hit them anymore anyway — or my gun barrel's crooked, one."

Helen turned to survey the packed boxes, the filled baskets.

"We've been torn up so long," she said of preparing for next Monday's sale, "I'm kind of anxious to get to the other house."

"We've got to go," Earl said. "We've sold this one, and the land."

THE GRAVESTONE

Of the many unusual stories I have gleaned from the beat that I cover, this one is among my favorites. A true account about a woman named Lucille (Lucy) Goodaker Franklin, it was told to me by her grandson, Charles L. Franklin, of Linton. He heard the narrative related by his mother on successive Decoration Days when they went to the cemetery to put flowers on family graves. It begins one day in May, a long time ago, with Lucy brooding over the recent death of a child.

As the sad events of the past few days flooded her mind, she was thankful for the spring sunshine. It warmed and soothed her while she sat on the doorstep of the three-room coal miner's house that was the Franklin home. Reliving the funeral of her little daughter, Edna, not quite six years old, who had succumbed so suddenly to meningitis, Lucy was trying desperately to remember the words of the minister who spoke so eloquently at the child's burial.

The wife of an Indiana coal miner, Lucy had known hard times. To earn a meager living for her and their family, her husband, Jim, worked fourteen hours a day in the mine, seven days a week; a half day on Sunday if he went to church. And there was never enough money to buy the things they needed. Living off coal was not an easy life.

Jim had missed a day's work so that he could attend his daughter's funeral. But he was back to work this day. Even though it was his own daughter who was dead, for the sake of the rest of his and Lucy's family, he could not afford to miss that day. No work, no pay was the rule of those early days, especially in the mines. Besides that, because of the war effort of 1918 the demand for coal was at an all time high.

Lucy's was a life of hard work. In addition to day-to-day demands, during the summer she would pick, clean and break, and can ninety quarts of string beans, or twice that many tomatoes, in a day's time. Despite that, she still would have supper on the table for Jim when he came in from his long day in the mine.

At the moment, she was resting on the limestone step of her house, absorbing the warm sunshine and thinking about little Edna's funeral. She remembered the friends who had come to say farewell to the child. She thought about the kind ladies of the Apostolic church who had cooked and fed her family. She remembered how sweetly they had sung her favorite hymn. They had been a great comfort to her.

She recalled, too, how after the funeral a broken-hearted Jim had promised to buy a stone marker for their little daughter's grave. She knew when she heard him that such a thing was an extravagance they could not afford, that a marker for the child's grave out of Jim's earnings was impossible.

What was it the preacher had said? It was coming back to her now. Something about a stepping stone. Oh yes. He said, "A grave is not a hole in the ground but a stepping stone to heaven."

As the words "stepping stone" flashed in her mind she realized what she was sitting on. A stepping stone! Suddenly she was filled with a great resolution. Her little Edna would indeed have a grave marker. Lucy got to her feet, walked into the house and returned with a hammer and a nail.

Incredibly, she began transforming the stepping stone that led to the doorway of little three-room miner's house into a grave marker. A few misses with the hammer hurt her fingers, but her purpose was greater than her pain. Slowly the limestone stepping stone yielded, and an epitaph began taking shape.

One evening in summer, after Jim had come home from the mine, they loaded the inscribed stepping stone into the wagon and took it to the cemetery. Barely readable, it is there yet today, in Fairview Cemetery, at Linton. It marks not only the grave of little Edna, but also the resolve of a loving wife and mother.

For another enjoyable book by Larry Incollingo, see the last page in this book. Send a gift copy to a loved one or to a friend.

THE JUDGE

On the way to visit Judge Samuel R. Rosen in the Brown County Courthouse one morning, I paused at the south entrance. There, I saw publicly honored on a memorial bronze plaque the number of countians who served in their country's wars: one thousand nine hundred and twenty-five.

This struck me as being an unusually large number for so small a county. Yet, beginning with ninety Brown countians who served in the Mexican War, and including five hundred seventy-five in the Civil War; eight in the Spanish-American War; three hundred and one in World War I; six hundred and sixty-four in World War II; one hundred and ninety-one in the Korean War; forty-seven in the Vietnam War; two in Panama; and forty-seven in the Persian Gulf; the total, in bronze, seemed indisputable.

Brown County's contribution to its country's past manpower commitments, however, is greater than that. According to additional information on the plaque, one hundred and fifty-two of those who answered the call to arms — fourteen in the Mexican War; ninety-six in the Civil War; twelve in World War I; twenty-two in World War II; seven in the Korean War; and one in the Vietnam War — lost their lives.

As impressive as the numbers on a bronze plaque was a "Roll of Honor" mounted in the entrance hall to the courthouse. To read the names as they appear in alphabetical order, to count them one by one, and to note the clusters of family names, such as fourteen Browns, ten Smiths, eight Foxes, eight Roberts, six Fleetwoods, and others, in World War II alone, the price small Brown County paid for those wars seemed to me to be incredibly high. Brown County should be proud of them.

Once a frequent stop on my beat, this was the first time I'd been in the Brown County Courthouse since its renovation. For that reason the new plaque and the refurbished Roll of Honor were new experiences for me. Had not newspapers recently carried an account of Judge Samuel Rosen's appointment by the Indiana Supreme Court as judge pro-tem of the Brown County Circuit Court, I might not have seen them at this time, for it was to congratulate him that I had gone there.

Still, my reason for being there went much deeper than mere congratulations. It was more because the realities of his life far surpassed even the dreams of so many of us that I went to see him. As a man he was simply amazing, and a detailed story of his life would make an interesting book. In lieu of that I made this brief sketch.

As an attorney serving as counsel to the draft board in Poughkeepsie, N.Y., during World War II, his name came up for induction into the Army. Because of his age, and because he was married and the father of three small children, he was eligible for a deferment; an offer he declined to accept.

In a matter of weeks after basic training he was in Europe, assigned to the 26th Infantry Division. Before the war was over, he had won the coveted Combat Infantryman Badge, three battle stars (one for the Battle of the Bulge), the bronze star, and for a wound he sustained in combat he was awarded the Purple Heart.

At the end of the war in Europe, when other soldiers were being discharged to their homes and families, he was detained. His Army MO had caught up with him and he was assigned to the Judge Advocate General's staff, serving in Germany until the end of 1945.

Judge Samuel R, Rosen

A graduate of Columbia and Harvard Law School, Judge Rosen at this time had been practicing law for more than sixty years. After a successful career in Poughkeepsie, he came to Indiana. During those early days here he was on the faculty at Notre Dame for two years, he also served as deputy attorney general of Indiana, and he was administrator-commissioner of the state supreme court.

He made his debut in Brown County almost a quarter century prior to this time as a retiree, but not really. He opened a small legal practice there. Then he ran successfully as a Democrat for circuit court judge, an office he held ten years.

In 1990 he retired a second time, but not really. He accepted an appointment as Senior Judge for Indiana. As such he traveled to various jurisdictions to fill in for judges who, for one reason or another, were temporarily unable to preside over their courts.

It was while he was serving in that capacity that Brown County Circuit Judge Judith A. Stewart was appointed U.S. Attorney for Southern Indiana, and he was tapped for that appointment.

At the time of this visit with him, at the tender age of eighty-three, Judge Rosen was back at his old bench, presiding over his old court, in a room filled with old memories.

It would last only a short time; Governor Evan Bayh was expected to appoint a new judge before the end of the year. When it would be over — well, it wouldn't be quite over. Not yet.

"I'm booked for a year after that as a senior judge," he told me during our visit. "I'll be pretty busy for a while."

Moreover, he hoped to author a sequel to his popular book, "A Judge Judges Mushrooms."

And then?

"Well," said the judge, "I intend to keep going for as long as I can. I think it's fatal when people stop working, when they stop doing what they can do. Besides that, work can be very interesting. There's not a day that goes by that you don't learn something new. It is the key to knowledge and intellectual curiosity."

Although he was only an adopted son, Brown County can be rightly proud of Judge Rosen. His name and life story ought to appear in a place of honor in the renovated courthouse, where it might serve as an inspiration to all men who see it.

VANGUARD OF EMPIRES

Had it not been for the existence of a small community newspaper more than a century ago, knowledge of one of Indiana's pioneers might never have come to light. Had history been so deprived, a model of courage and fearlessness would have been denied generations of Hoosier women.

It was not until her death that the story of Sallie White was told. Occurring more than a hundred years ago, it was reported in the *Leesville Sun*, published January 30, 1879, in the frontier community of Leesville, in Lawrence County.

Sallie — now the legendary "Granny" White of Spring Mill State Park — lived courageously, fearlessly and long enough to catch the eye of an unknown but discerning obituary writer. It is only because he or she did such a remarkable job of it that Granny, since her demise, has become a standard of strength and determination among Indiana women familiar with her story.

Sallie Cummins White was born in 1874 in Connecticut and later moved with her parents to the Catskills region of New York. There the girl Sallie grew to the respectable age of nineteen and married Silas Sutherland. Accompanied by Sallie's mother, they journeyed to Canada and settled near Toronto.

Six children were born to the couple in their years there. When the territory began filling up after the War of 1812, Silas and Sallie decided to return to the U.S. Leaving Granny Cummins behind, they loaded some wagons with their belongings, and their six children, and left Canada. Rather than go back to Connecticut or any other heavily populated area, they headed their wagons for the extreme frontier of that period — Indiana.

A side note that is of some interest involves a bit of palm tickling at the U.S.-Canadian border; William, one of the six children, paid a border guard a half dollar to pass the wagon he was driving without inspecting it, thereby managing to smuggle duty-free into the U.S. a number of guns.

The long journey was not completed without a series of setbacks. The worst occurred on the trip southward through Ohio. Silas became ill and died. Sallie suddenly found herself the sole provider and protector of her large family.

The obituary writer, seizing on what must have been a difficult time for Sallie, wrote of her loss on the trail in this fashion:

"You mothers who have never wanted for the common comforts of life, friends or neighbors, can hardly realize the condition of that widow and her six fatherless children, almost alone in the solitude of the formidable forest with so fresh a grief.

"Without a single qualm, help or strength, save that from her own resources, (and) on an obscure highway, the elevated plateau of southwestern Ohio and Indiana, with deep ravines and swift streams without bridges or ferries, and many miles intervening, she resolved to continue; no turning back, no fainting.

"That strong inflexible purpose to secure a home stilled her weeping heart, and the sight of her children nerved her to action. Here was the character that forms the vanguard of empires."

Sallie was a special kind of woman. One worthy of the respect and honor attributed to her memory. But the story doesn't end there. When the family reached Vallonia, in Jackson County, Sallie decided to follow the East Fork of White River south. When they came to the tiny settlement of Sparksville, they stopped. The resourceful Sallie was able to come up with enough money and possessions to make a deal for a piece of land, and they spent the winter there.

When spring came Sallie married David White, and they set about building a two-story log house on the Bloomington Road, about a quarter mile north of Leesville. When it was completed, husband and wife saddled their horses and with pack horses trailing, they rode to Toronto to bring back Sallie's mother, Granny Cummins. On their return to Indiana, Sallie settled down and had three children by David.

Sallie was a Calvanistic Baptist, the obituary read. "As a neighbor (she was) neighborly (and) charitable in all things, benevolent to her own injury, kind and affable in manner and conversation, genteel and modest, steadfast in her faith, and respected and mourned by a host of lineal and collateral kindred and friends."

The obituary listed the cause of her death, which was diagnosed as pneumonia, and that she died at the age of 95 at the home of Euretta Hall. It was not until some four decades later that the life of Sallie White, so impressively eulogized by the unknown obituary writer, was found to be not without historic meaning.

Her life story was recorded for posterity and what remained of the two story log house she and David White had built was removed to Spring Mill State Park. There it was restored and furnished, and still occupies a place of prominence in the park's Old Village. Although many of the thousands who have since visited the home have been women, many remain unaware of her contribution to the courage and nobility of womankind.

ED'S

There was a time when from as far west as Trenton, Illinois, and east to Versailles, Indiana, road signs, a hundred or more of them, used to call attention to "Ed's Ghost Town." Their black-on-white messages read, "Ed's Ghost Town, 170 miles," or "Ed's Indian Jewelry, 90 miles," or "Ed's Baskets, 50 miles," or "Ed's Moccasins...." Ed's, on U. S. 50 between Bedford and Shoals, is no more. How come? It's a long story. In a nutshell, its demise was the result of highway closings.

Ed and Evelyn Hirsch had opened Ed's in 1950, not too long after he, a fellow from Iowa, and she, a girl from Ohio, met for the first time at an ice skating rink in Indianapolis. Four years later "Ed's" signs began appearing; four of them that year. And Ed's was on its way to a measure of success.

Ed and Evelyn's dream, "That we'd have a big tourist attraction for southern Indiana," was in the making. But the dream was never quite completed. The first indication that it might not ever be realized came in 1958 when U. S. 50 east of Ed's was closed for repairs.

"When they close this highway there is nothing you can do about it," Ed said at the time. "And when they close it we feel the pinch."

The pinch moved Ed to try harder. More signs were made, and from the store west and east they appeared on land rented at a cost of five dollars to twenty dollars annually. By the early 1960's some one hundred of them beckoned to motorists driving between St. Louis and Cincinnati: "Ed's . . ."

Ed also bounded back from that first road closing with Ed's Ghost Town. It was comprised of nine buildings erected on a hilly wooded tract behind the large building that had become Ed's. He had a false-fronted hotel, saloon, jail, hardware store, and other pioneer-town type buildings.

It flourished, but only briefly. For it was about that time that the popular TV western began to wane, and with it went any interest in ghost towns of any kind. Transient traffic past Ed's was still considerable enough to make the big shop profitable. Luckily. For by then Ed and Evelyn had four more mouths to feed: four sons.

The good times came to an abrupt halt again in 1966 with the installation of a new bridge on U. S. 50 between Shoals and Loogootee.

"The detour lasted for a long time," Ed remembered. "And when that happens out here you hurt. We hurt."

It happened again in 1973: another new bridge, another detour, another hurt.

"Those closings lasted an average of five months," Ed said. "And each of them came at a time when we expected our best business of the year. We knew it could happen, but it was really the failure of the highway that got us."

The U. S. 50 blacktop west of the sprawling building that was Ed's simply slipped its mooring and pitched over the south shoulder of the road. The cave-in made travel in that immediate area possible only via a detour over a county road — and that on a pitching hillside — that connected U. S. 50 with State Road 60 between Spice Valley and Mitchell.

However, detour signs appeared at the junction of U. S. 50 and State Road 37, miles east of Ed's, and at U. S. 50 and State Road 60 west of Ed's. In both instances through traffic, vital to Ed's, was directed through Mitchell, many miles from the store.

Local traffic soon learned of a shorter — unmarked — detour; the "illegal" detour, some folks called it.

Ed Hirsch

But transients were detoured long before they ever reached that point.

"Our business went down to nothing," Ed said. "The road was closed from October until sometime in April. If our dream was coming true, those months destroyed it. And we concluded that our livelihood, no matter how hard we might try, was dependent upon situations completely beyond our control.

"When spring came, we made our decision. We decided we'd close Ed's and do something else."

That's most of the story, but not quite the end of it. Nor was it the end of Ed and Evelyn's dream; that was a kind of continuing thing, in spite of setbacks. It continued in this manner.

During a visit to the home of a relative in Ohio, Evelyn became acquainted with Shaklee products. After the U. S. 50 cave-in, the Hirsches investigated Shaklee possibilities. They went to a couple of meetings, heard success stories, and decided to try their luck.

Why not? Ed's, for all of the business it was doing, or it wasn't doing, depending on your point of view, might as well have been shut down. They invested twelve dollars and fifty cents in a Shaklee kit, studied it, and began using Shaklee products. Then, by following a prescribed sales method, they began attracting other people to Shaklee. Soon they became supervisors with forty people signed up. And before long they had done enough business to make them eligible to go to a Shaklee convention in San Francisco.

But that's not all. Ed and Evelyn also sold enough Shaklee to win themselves a free new automobile. And they were looking forward to receiving a Shaklee bonus check in the amount of eleven hundred dollars.

"It's not near as much as we earned in the store in our best years, 1970 and 1971," noted Ed. "But it will get even better."

Ed and Evelyn had their sights set on becoming Master Coordinators; supervising fifteen persons who were expected to do what they had already done. Their bonus checks were then expected to run from eight thousand to twelve thousand dollars a month, and they would drive a free new Cadillac or Lincoln Continental, Ed said.

"I'm suffering no remorse over our broken dream," he said. "Neither is Evelyn. It's really not broken. Because we still have a dream. This new challenge."

Had it not been for the road closings, the Hirsches might never have come to this point. Ed's as travelers from the fifty states had known it, is no more. And the road signs from as far west as Trenton, Illinois, and east to Versailles, Indiana, that read "Ed's . . . ," unless one has been overlooked someplace along the way, are forever gone from view.

LORENE WHITE

One cold February evening in 1922 a young woman stood up in the Handy Church in Monroe County and announced to the minister and the gathered worshipers her wish to be baptized.

When the trap door leading to the baptismal tank, installed under the church floor, was opened, a shocking discovery was made. Hot fires in two heating stoves, one at either end of the church, had been no match for the cold outside. A thick layer of ice covered the water in the tank.

"They had to chop the ice away so that I could be baptized," that woman recounted the experience to me one day a lifetime later. "It was cold, all right. But I had made my mind up. I wanted to be baptized, and I was."

On the way home from church she was admonished by her husband who was fearful that immersion in the ice cold water would prove to be a fatal mistake.

"You shouldn't have done it. You are going to catch pneumonia and die," he worriedly scolded. "In the morning I am going to leave you. I cannot live with a Christian."

Not only was she still alive in the morning, her husband hadn't left. And they continued as man and wife, living almost fifty-five happy years together before he passed away. At the time of my visit with her, she was ninety-five and the oldest member of her church. White-haired, bespectacled, exuding warmth and congeniality, she seemed a glittering star in a dimming universe.

"I know what I got when I gave my heart to the Lord, and I know when I got it," she said in summation of that cold dunking back in 1922 and her life since then.

She had challenged the cold before. On the way to school one winter morning, years before her baptism, it was so cold that a heavy frost that lay over everything in sight appeared to be as thick as a light snow. "We were so poor we had no shoes or socks," she remembered. "And when my little brother complained of being cold I sat him down on the ground beside me and wrapped his feet in my dress tail."

This wonderful lady's name was Lorene White. When I telephoned to interview her at her Main Street home in Sanders, she apologized that she was cramped for time. Her morning, she informed me, would be taken with two gooseberry pies she had promised to bake for a friend, but she would be free in the afternoon.

"Baking pies!" she exclaimed at my later query. "I've always done it. If I had all the pies I have baked since I was fourteen, I would have a roadstand and hire somebody to sell all those pies for me. And I'd make so much money that I would have a big limousine with a chauffeur, and I would travel around the world. I've baked all kinds of pies, and I've baked them for relatives and friends. I love to do it. And, she added proudly, "I never bought a crust in my life."

She believed she had been put on this earth to help people, and that was one of the reasons she had baked so much. She also did washings and ironings for people when they were sick and in need of help. She had always believed that if she ever needed their help they would reciprocate. Trouble was, she had out-lived them all.

Lorene is her middle name. She prefers it over her first name which is actually "Easter," a name given to her in honor of the Feast of the Resurrection, the day on which she was born — Easter Sunday morning in 1902.

Because of the method of determining the date of Easter, she had celebrated only two Easter Sunday birthday anniversaries since then. Once when Easter Sunday came on March 30 in 1975 and the other March 30, 1996.

It was the scarcity of those anniversaries that prompted her husband, Jim, one day, to promise her the time of her life on that approaching anniversary in 1975.

"No matter how much it costs, no matter how long it takes me to pay for it," he would repeatedly promise, "we are going to celebrate. We are going out."

"He had made plans for our outing," she said. "He never told me what they were. My birthday was Easter Sunday, March 30, 1975. He died on March 8. It made me feel awfully sad. He used to come up behind me while I was at the stove and slip his arms around me and sing, 'Darling we are growing old, silver threads among the gold.' I sure do miss him."

She and Jim had four children. The three who were still living were loving and visited or kept in touch regularly. Memories of a deceased daughter still brought pain.

"I found out you can give up mother, father, or brother, but their loss is nothing compared to the loss you suffer when you have to give up a child," she said. "Oh, you never get over something like that. And I miss her so much."

Except for the losses, life — the Lord, as she preferred to say — had been good to her, was still good to her. Though most of those friends of her generation had passed on, there were many other people, in addition to her children, who also loved her.

"If I'm in the shower or the bath tub, the telephone rings," she began a litany of their almost daily concern for her. "If I'm washing my hair, or if I'm up to my elbows in pie dough, or I'm watching something I want to see real bad on television, the telephone rings. I'll excuse myself and say, 'Can you call me back, my coffee is going to get cold,' and I go to get more coffee. But before I can pour it the telephone rings again. If I go into the bedroom, the telephone rings. There are so many people who worry about me and are so good to me," she said amusingly pleased.

When I asked about her plans for the future, Easter Lorene White replied, "I'm going to try my best to continue living for the Lord. It's a happy life living for Him. I want Him to hold on to me for a little while longer. I've come too far to slip back now."

For an autographed copy of one of Larry Incollingo's other books, please turn to the back of this book.

MEDORA: A MEMORY

I was rather surprised to see the horizontal lines of a staff on which there were three notes on the red-on-blue sign that greeted my arrival at Medora in Jackson County. "An itinerant music teacher by the name of West Lee Wright," explained school principal William Spray, "named the town. You remember the notes do, re, me? Well, he's supposed to have rearranged those notes to read 'me', 'do', 'ra' for the name of this town." Well, I suppose that's all right. Although I couldn't help but wonder why Wright chose to spell the second tone of the scale ra instead of re. But ra or re took nothing away from the town which natives described as being a "town of harmony," and "old fashioned, but streamlined."

"It owes its origins to agriculture," Spray told me. "This is all good farmland here, and after the railroad came through people moved down from Weddlesville, west of here, to be near the railroad."

Spray had been teaching for thirty-six years. A slim, genial man, who also farmed two hundred and fifty acres and owned thirty milk cows, he held the distinction of having been principal of the only township school to survive consolidation.

Carr Township School then had an enrollment of nearly three hundred pupils from K through twelve, with less than one hundred of those being in the twelfth grade.

Spray's ancestors came up the Ohio and eventually settled in Jackson County. The community that grew up around them was named Spraytown. Only a couple dozen people were there at this time, but the name could be found on a road sign there and on an old road map, as may be found the names Acme and

Surprise, two other settlements which were near to Spraytown.

I met Spray quite by accident, while I was studying a small painting of the longest covered bridge in any one state in the United States which hung on a landing wall in his school.

My purpose for being where I was at the time was the bridge, but on this first visit ever to Medora, I found the place so interesting I decided to approach the bridge in a roundabout fashion.

Someone once described Medora as "a nice little old country town" of brick and frame dwellings and mobile homes, where school children play basketball on outdoor courts, and baseball and softball at recess. It was a town of perhaps eight hundred souls, complete with bank, grocery stores, package store, tavern and pool room.

"In the heart of Medora," as it was advertised in the old hotel building, a lady named Carrie Kinder operated the town's most prominent independent restaurant, Ye Ol' Kountry Kitchen.

"This place was the Medora Hotel years ago," Carrie explained, "but over the years it became just 'the old hotel.'"

Before she took it over and remodeled the first floor into the handsome restaurant that it was, Hiram Smith had the building, and he kept it full of antiques and junk, she said.

The old hotel had a history, and Carrie had a photograph which showed its founder and the founder's daughter. And she had a memory, too, about the old hotel — a memory of a killing there. But Carrie would have had to have shown you the photo, and told you about the killing — while you were eating baked ham, roast beef, steak or fried chicken. That was part of the mystique of the place. Fried chicken was a big favorite at the Kountry Kitchen. "Because," Carrie explained its success, "I fry it in a skillet, and I keep frying it as long as there's anyone here to eat it."

Breakfast and lunch patrons usually were from the town or surrounding area, but dinner generally brought outsiders who had learned of the Kountry Kitchen's home-cooked foods cooked by Mabel Gibson.

Carrie was one of those rare people who could make you feel welcome without trying. She was reared on a river bottom farm just east of town, in the first house on the right after you cross the new bridge, where Wayne Howell lived.

Her father and Victor Turmail at one time were the richest farmers in the White River Valley, she said. Ralph Wolka, her father, and Marietta Meahl Wolka, her mother, were frugal German farmers who provided a good home and a productive farm for their four children.

Carrie remembered a single lavish expenditure by her father — a trip to St. Louis by Greyhound Bus to go to the fair.

"We all hung barefooted on the fence and cried the day he left," she remembered. "We could see the bus coming — a cloud of dust on old U.S. 50.

"It was always an occasion to see it go by," she said. "It was the largest thing on the road. And it stopped at every house. But on that day it was something else. Our father was going to get on it and go all the way to St. Louis.

"My father was not a kisser," she choked up a little as she bordered on the sentimental, "but he kissed us that day — each one of us goodbye. And I remember my mother telling him, 'I'll see you when you get back.'

"I can see him now," she said, "with his felt hat on. He always wore a felt hat. And that bus, with a motor sticking out in front, and the pull-down shades."

Home-brew in a German home was as traditional as it was commonplace when Carrie was growing up. And children as well as adults drank it. She remembered that her mother would halt her labors over a hot iron on a board and split a bottle of home-brew with her children, and that "When Grandma died at ninety-two, there was only one thing she wanted before she passed on — a cold brew."

It naturally followed that on her first date Carrie should ask for a bottle of beer instead of a Coke.

"I never heard of Coke," she said. "And there I was with a real good Methodist fellow who played a horn in the choir."

William Spray remembered when drummers got off the B & O passenger trains and put up at the hotel. A livery to the rear of the hotel provided them with horses and buggies and they toured the countryside selling their wares.

"And anyone over fifty remembers U. S. 50 when it came through here, and how everyone wanted to see if his car could make the Knobbs west of here in high gear," Spray said.

"I can remember, when I was a boy I'd rarely go up there but what there weren't one or two cars hung up there. And there were always rocks in the road that somebody had used to chock his car with," he recalled.

The Medora Knobbs rise sharply to the west, and although the climb was a sightseer's delight, I found myself thankful that I wasn't making it in a car, or bus, fifty years ago.

I asked Spray why Medora had never consolidated with other Jackson County township schools, and his answer was quite simple.

"Everyone around here has been too contrary to consolidate," he said with a happy smile.

The covered bridge to which I referred earlier was situated on State Road 235, about a mile or so east of Medora and spans the East fork of White River where Mahan's ferry once operated. It was one of southern Indiana's famous historical landmarks, having had the distinction of being the longest covered bridge in the USA, in any one state.

It was opened to travel Saturday, July 17, 1875, and was closed a couple of years before my visit when the new bridge replacing it was opened.

"A million dollar bridge," Wayne Howell had said of the new span, "and you can't get to it."

Arcing high over the East Fork of White River the new span rose from a river bottom blacktop, leaving the bridge's approaches under water when the river left its banks.

The new bridge didn't cost a million; a couple hundred thousand shy of that amount. However functional it may or may not have been in periods of high water, alongside the old bridge it did provide a contrast of the old and the new.

One Jackson County Courthouse official said of the old covered bridge that, "The state is going to dump it on to the county, and I mean dump, because I don't know what we'd want with it."

Joe Persinger, then News Editor of the Brownstown Banner, however, told me that the bridge already belonged to the county, and that the county was turned down for a forty thousand dollar grant under HUD's 1974 Community Development Act, dashing a hope that the county might re-roof three of its covered bridges, including the one at Medora.

Then county commissioners Harry Schepman, Delmar Ault and Earl Goecker also favored the establishment of riverside parks near the old bridges, but in the case of the Medora covered bridge the state

Derelict longest covered bridge at Medora.

pulled a weirdo. It gave the county the old bridge but kept the land around it.

"The county wasn't too thrilled about that," Joe told me.

Generally, the people of Medora would have liked the old bridge preserved for posterity, and the land around it developed into a riverside park.

One of those was Sheryl Price. Mrs. Price was actively engaged in the promotion of the bridge restoration and the Jack-Law Trail, a foot, bike and horse trail past the bridge and over the scenic Medora Knobbs in Jackson County and the Devil's Backbone in Lawrence County.

Her interest in the old bridge flared when she became aware of people tearing boards off the bridge to use for wall hangings and picture frames. Her husband, Robert, was a member of the town's three-man board and, with Joe Campbell and Jim Fish, the other two members, once entertained the hope that funds might be obtained to save the old relic.

On a wall in the living room of the two-story brick house that had been in Mrs. Price's family ever since she could remember, there was a tinted, blown-up photograph of the east end of the bridge which was made by her brother Frank Roger Davis.

Davis completed the handsome print in 1972 and a copy of his work hung in the offices of the Medora State Bank.

Another blow-up that hung in the bank was taken from a black and white photograph made by Spray.

Spray was another advocate of the bridge restoration program. The 24X30 inch color enlargement of his photo of the bridge was one of two such reproductions of the old bridge. He planned to have three more made.

It was while I was studying Charles Eshon's painting of the old bridge in the school, that I met William Spray. He told me Eshon was handicapped and that he had ridden out to the bridge in a buggy, the only way he had of getting around, to do the painting in 1890.

The long bridge — four hundred and sixty-two feet — was constructed of three spans supported by inside arches that measure ninety feet each.

When it was built by J. J. Daniels in 1874-75 it cost a mere eighteen thousand one hundred and forty-two dollars.

When it was learned the old landmark was to be bypassed by a new bridge, Clyde Lingle Gilbert was inspired to do a painting of the old bridge, and to compose the following three-stanza poem in honor of its service.

"The Old Covered Bridge is still holding on.
Landmark of rare beauty, soon may be gone.
Having faithfully carried man, wagon and steed —
But not fast enough, for today's super speed.

"Covered bridge builders were crafters of skill,
Shaping and fitting huge timbers at will.
Manual labor those days set a trend,
More than a century before automation began.

"Farewell Covered Bridge, it's like losing a friend.
Thousands will miss you on to the end.
You've done a good job by serving us well,
Leaving true reminiscences for history to tell."

GERALD AND THELMA

Down where Nob Creek flanks one side of a shaded summer blacktop, and Covey Ridge rises a half mile above the other, children, one day, frolicked in a muddy swimming hole. In the cool of a mammoth beech tree, Gerald and Thelma Sowder entertained on their nearby patio.

It was morning, already hot and humid, but comfortable under the big beech. And Thelma, comfortable in her bare feet, imparted a soaring dimension to the ease and freedom of that place.

"I love it," Gerald said. "We've been here forty-seven years. It feels like home to us. We've got family all around."

A daughter, Maxine, lived next door. A son, Harold, lived nearby. Son Farrell lived only a few miles away in Bedford. Daughter Barbara resided on State Road 58. Sister Carolyn had a home on the Williams Road. Irene, most distant from Nob Creek, lived at Switz City.

The rest of the family included nineteen grandchildren and twenty-three great grandchildren. The youngsters cutting capers in the creek were great grandchildren.

"When the whole family gets together — counting in-laws, out-laws and whatever — there are more than sixty of us," Gerald said with obvious satisfaction. He smiled largely and observed, "That's a bunch."

Gerald, who was looking forward to his nearing seventy-third birthday anniversary had been retired from Central Foundry in Bedford for thirteen years.

"I had a good job," he said. "But I made up my mind to retire and I couldn't wait to get out. The last three months were the longest of my life. But I finally got out, with good health, and I'm enjoying every minute."

78

Gerald and Thelma Sowder

Joyful minutes were spent doing many things, including fishing from a bass boat in Lake Monroe, tending two vegetable gardens, cutting winter firewood, hunting, and shooting pool on a regulation table in a room behind the Sowder's two-car garage.

"The boys (sons, sons-in-law, grandsons) and I get together back here," he said of the large room. "We spend many hours together and have a good time. One of my daughters gave me this pool table for Christmas one year."

A large freezer and a refrigerator occupied one corner. A wood range in another corner was the source of delicious home cooking. A "No Smoking" sign hung from a wall, and an electric clock that ran backwards hung above that.

"When there is nothing else to do I'll tune my chain saws," Gerald smiled at the recollection of a popular complaint against retirees. "One thing for sure, no one can say that I get underfoot."

The children, their hair wet and stringy, had come up from the creek. Great Grandfather and Great Grandmother gave them requested attention.

"They have a great time playing in the water," Gerald observed. "But I'll never understand how. Nob Creek is fed by underground springs and the water is so cold it will pretty near cut rings around you."

The cold water emptied into Little Salt Creek not

too distant from the Sowder home. From there Little Salt sliced through woodlands and broad farmlands in the Logan Bottoms and into Big Salt Creek. The latter merged with the East Fork of White River above Williams.

Gerald was born and reared in the Nob Creek neighborhood. He traveled to Bartlettsville to school, repeating both the seventh and eighth grades there.

"I was smart in my books," he remembered. "But I just didn't want to go to high school, which was in Heltonville. My teacher, Ernest Winklepeck, who was also the undertaker, just begged me to go to high school. But I wouldn't do it."

Fifty-four years earlier, Gerald and Thelma had ridden nine miles to Bedford to the office of J. V. Stapp, Justice of the Peace. There, in the view of witnesses Beryl Covey, a friend, and Birtle Sowder, Gerald's father, they were married. Seven years later they moved to Nob Creek and at this time were celebrating their forty-seventh year there.

"But not in the same house," Gerald noted. "One Sunday morning in March, twenty-four years ago, our house was destroyed by fire. We came this way some and dug a basement and built this house," he nodded in the direction of the white frame to which the shaded patio was attached. "We like it awfully well. It's home to us."

In Gerald's words, it also felt like home. The gleeful noises of Sowder great grandchildren coasting downhill on a bicycle, and the clear and sharp call of a bob white quail gave it the sound of home.

"We just love it," Thelma smiled. "We've got everything we ever wanted right here. And we have a really nice country church up on the ridge."

It was just luck (with a little help from farmers working by a roadside close by) that I found the

Sowder home. It would have been impossible to direct anyone to it. Luckily I made a note of the route Gerald gave me to get out of Nob Creek, which, if you'd like to go there, could be taken in reverse.

"Go out here to the T, and turn right," he instructed in the route to take from there. "At the next T turn left and go 'til you come to a Y, and turn right. Cross the creek and turn back to the right, cross the railroad, climb Inman Hill and go straight into Old (Ind.) 37 at Judy (Judah)."

Good luck.

FRANK SOUTHERN

As Frank and Wanda Southern's wedding anniversary was approaching, Frank confided to this reporter that he was looking forward not only to it, their sixtieth, but he said with a smile of assurance, "I'm shooting for more."

Frank and Wanda were married on Christmas Day in 1917. "In," as Frank remembered it, "a little old house on East Seventh Street in Bloomington," by a minister whose name was James A. Thrasher.

"They've since torn the place down," Frank said. Then he joked, "When I saw that happen I said, 'Well now we can dissolve the marriage.'"

In the next breath, after explaining on the telephone to Wanda that he was being interviewed by a reporter, he promised with mellow enthusiasm, "I'll call you later, Honey."

After hanging up he said to me, "There's no question that the best thing that ever happened to me is having a wife like her for these many years."

It was in the later years of Paul and Tulia Taylor's Coffee Cup restaurant at 111 South Walnut Street in Bloomington that Frank and I became friends. He took coffee there of a morning and at the time I was a tea drinker. There were others: Earl Hudelson, John Kleindorfer, Wayne Carmichael, Lowell Wagner, Vic Settle, Dale Schreiber, Lloyd Brown, Francis Baker, Marje Robinson, John Headley, Jimmy Hall, Byron Haas, and city and county policemen, and others.

The Coffee Cup was a hole in the wall-size eatery, and its counter, in the shape of a carpenter's square, accommodated at a given time a maximum of thirteen patrons. The little restaurant's advertising slogan was, "Seating capacity thirteen thousand, thirteen at a time." It was a cozy place and numerous friendships were made and flourished there.

When Paul and Tulia closed its door for the last time on July 4, 1969, the loss was painful. To utter a commonplace, yet never a truer statement, its closing was like the passing of an old friend.

Frank was just a young fellow when we met there; he was only sixty-eight. At that time he'd been around Bloomington for awhile. He arrived in the city as a youngster from Rush Ridge, in Salt Creek Township, Monroe County, which is now on the shores of Lake Monroe. A memory from there he carried with him was one of the sale of two thousand acres of land which sold for a dollar an acre.

Romey and Laura Deckard Southern brought their three children, Grant, Goldie (Volk), and Frank to a better life in Bloomington. But Romey, who fired five boilers at the old Indiana University heating plant, lived to enjoy only a brief share of it. Frank was eleven at the time of his father's death, and it wasn't long afterward that a lifetime of work was to begin for him.

Early in that period he met Ben Becovitz, and went to work for him at the Louben. Ladies wear was available on the first floor of the Louben, old timers will recall, and Frank sold men's wear in the basement level of the store.

"That," Frank remembered, "was when you could buy a good suit of clothes for fifteen dollars."

After three years with the Louben, the opportunity of his life came Frank's way. With an assist from Ben, Frank applied to the Monroe County State Bank to fill a bookkeeping vacancy there, and he was accepted.

That was in 1918, and Frank was there for the rest of his life. But not as a bookkeeper. At this time he was marking his fifty-ninth year there. He remembered Ben with a fondness that was as fresh as it was then.

"He was just a wonderful fellow," he said of Ben. "If there is a second 'best' thing that's happened in my life," he added, "it's having had the privilege of knowing Ben Becovitz." And then with obvious dignity he said, "I have to thank God, too, for the fine people who have come into my life who have treated me so well — like Ben."

It wasn't entirely receiving that enriched his life. Frank also gave. In addition to leading and influencing the growth of the bank, he served as the chairman of the Salvation Army Board for twenty-five years; he was the first president of the Central Lions Club which he helped charter in 1928; he served as chairman of the Red Cross for twenty years; he was a member of the school board; and he served twenty years on the city's parks and recreation board, and he also was a member of the Church of Christ for twenty-five years.

The city of Bloomington on November 24, 1968, dedicated the Frank Southern Center on South Henderson Street to his service. On other occasions he was presented a number of civic commendations, among them the Exchange Club's coveted Book of Golden Deeds. There were other cherished awards, such as the words of one man which were also those of many others:

"Thank you, Frank, for the help you gave me in getting the mortgage on my house," he said.

And those Monroe County Bank employees who spoke for themselves and their co-workers: "Everybody just loves him," John Kleindorfer said. "He is a real nice person. He has been like a father to me."

"We all just love him," Ada Brock, who had spent thirty years working with Frank, said. "He's a wonderful person. He's more like a buddy than an employer."

"There's just no one better," said Grace Bushert, who had worked at the bank for twenty-five years. "Frank's the nicest person you could ever want to meet."

"He's one of the finest individuals I've ever met," said Tom Risen, then assistant vice president. "There's not a malicious bone in his entire body."

And to cap them all were the words of Honey, whom he told over the phone he would call later: "We've had a wonderful life together," Wanda said from the Southern home at 614 North College Avenue. "The years with him have been happy years. I couldn't ask for anything more."

Frank was aware of none of this when from behind his desk — the one with the nameplate that read "Chairman Emeritus" — he said, "I'm so happy that I've been able to work with all these people. I could never have accomplished what I have in my lifetime if I had not had the support of friends and the people of the community."

He recalled an illness in 1942 from which he was surprised to recover.

"And suddenly here I am," he said gratefully, "I'm eighty years old, I've been married sixty years, and I've been in the bank fifty-nine years. I've enjoyed life. I still enjoy life," and a big smile filled his face and eyes as he added, "I'd like to live a little longer."

REQUIEM FOR CHARLIE

A recent afternoon in Orleans, while Wayne Freed and Gene Compton were gabbing in Elmo Wolfe's Barber Shop, Wayne looked at his watch and observed, "Well, Gene, it looks like Charlie"s probably not going to show up. We might as well go get our coffee."

A klatch had been meeting at Elmo's, then walking up to Herle's Cafe. Of late, old age and illness had been hacking away at its numbers. More recently, in late September, one of them died: Charlie Ragsdale. And like Wayne said, he probably wouldn't show up for coffee that day.

At the barber shop last Tuesday, some of us extended Wayne's requiem for Charlie. We remembered the man who used to make us smile, the man who sometimes made us laugh so hard our bellies shook, the man who was so good for us.

Charlie was good for Charlie, too. His humor kept him bright and smiling and belied his years. Once, as we shared cherry cobbler at Herle's, he said of being an octogenarian, "I'm really not that old, I've just been around that long."

Still smiling he added, "I try not to let my age bother me." Remembering his wife, Ethel, whose last days were spent in a nursing home, Charlie said somberly, "But sometimes it worries me. I wouldn't want to be confined like that."

He was, unhappily. But fortunately for those who loved him, he was in a nursing home for only a matter of weeks. Had he a choice he probably would have preferred his last moments to have found him standing at a number one tee, announcing with a smile as he always did to his golfing companions, "This is where friendship ceases — and hell begins."

In his good friend's barber shop one morning

Charlie confided in mock despair, "I'm lucky to shoot under a hundred." Then loud enough so that the working Elmo could hear, he added, "I play the town barber a lot. I've only beat him twice. After that he got ugly and made me give him a stroke." He smiled and winked, "He's so ugly, when he was born the doctor slapped his mother."

Charlie was a born story teller. No matter how many years a story had been around, when he repeated it, it was funny. Like the one about the devoted golfer who took time from his game to remove his hat and bow his head in deference to a passing funeral procession.

"Someone you know?" his partner asked.

"Tomorrow," the man replied as he resumed his game, "we'd have been married thirty-five years."

Charlie's humor followed him almost to the grave. During the eulogy at his funeral in Bethel Church near Orangeville, the preacher told the gathered mourners, "Charlie was a teller of tales. Trouble is," the minister said, "we can't tell some of them here."

Most of Charlie's tales were tellable anyplace. Many were unashamedly churchy. Elmo, who helped carry his good friend to his grave, remembered one Charlie told about the parishioner who fell asleep during the sermon.

"Wake him up," the preacher called to an usher.

"You wake him up," the usher countered. "You put him to sleep."

Then there was Charlie's story about the survey-taking clergyman.

"Are you Christian?" the story begins with a minister speaking to a householder.

"Nope," the man replied. "Christian lives next door."

The minister shook his head. "No, no. I mean, do you read the Bible?"

"Nope. Can't read," the man answered.

"Well then," the minister persisted, "are you ready for the Judgement?"

"When is it?" the man asked.

"Tomorrow, maybe," said the minister. "Maybe next day."

The man scratched his head. "In that case," he drawled, "I'd better go inside and tell the old woman. Knowing her, she'll probably want to go both days."

Someone once said that story-telling was Charlie's claim to fame. It was but one. Before his retirement to Orleans he was also a successful Orangeville farmer. He was a loving husband and father, too. He was a good brother to six siblings. Having been blessed with a good voice and heart, he made the time to sing at something like seven hundred weddings and funerals. His credits go on and on.

He once said of Elmo's barber shop, "It's a good place to spend time. I have a lot of friends who go there, Democrats and Republicans. There's a lot of difference between them, you know. Democrats are pretty good people. I think we're all good friends, though."

Seriously he added, "It doesn't matter what we are, for when we get to where we're going we'll all be united brethren."

Charlie was eighty-three when he died. Some months before he had to go to the nursing home he confided to Elmo what, he said, was his dearest wish for his passing.

"I've never made much of a contribution to society," he told Elmo. "But I would at least like to leave a pleasant memory when I go."

REVA'S

I surveyed again the lady who had prepared the chicken lying thick and tender amid large yellow noodles on the plate before me, the mashed potatoes smothered in gravy and the garden peas, and I shuddered at the words she had uttered:

"I had my heart set on being a school teacher."

Reva Weekly, fortunately, could not afford college. She became instead of a teacher, a restaurateur, although it is doubtful that she'd have used that word in the small Hoosier community of Freetown.

She ran the restaurant there, the only one. And she'd been running it for twenty-six years, although as the years passed she did so with some modification.

"On basketball game nights we'd stay open waiting for the buses to come back. Sometimes until midnight and after. And then there'd be standing room only until everybody was fed," she spoke the memory almost fondly.

"I used to open at six in the morning and close at midnight, or after the game crowd was fed. But not anymore," she said with a shake of her head.

Freetown was small enough to have lost its high school to consolidation. With the games gone there were no crowds. With the kids gone there was little reason to remain open for the long hours. And Reva cut them back, again and again. The last time was to the bone; and at this time Reva's place was open daily only from 11 a.m. 'til 2 p.m.

"It takes as long to prepare food for these short hours," she said. "You have to get up just as early to prepare for a three-hour lunch as you would to stay open all day. But the long hours are gone. I don't have to stay here all night anymore."

If the loss to consolidation brought her as a restaurateur any pain, Reva did not reveal it. After more than a quarter century of serving food from the same stand, she would admit to no regrets.

"I've tried to be good to this business," she said with satisfaction. "I just hope it's been that good to me. I'm not sure it has yet."

One of her rewards was that she had labored at home, or close to home. Reared near Kurtz, she went to grade school at Clear Spring and graduated from Houston High School.

"More than twenty of us started our senior year but only eleven of us graduated. It was hard for folks to keep their kids in school back then; there was so little money around," she said, noting a sad fact of life in the late 1930s.

Had there been even a little money available to her, college might have been possible, she would have become a teacher, as she had hoped, and good eating in Freetown would have been the loser.

"We were aware of the value of education all right. My great grandfather was a professor at Mooney College in Clear Spring. But when I graduated from high school, there was just no way that we could afford any more schooling," she said explaining the eating world's gain.

She remembered that Mooney, in its time, had turned out teachers, and that scholars arrived there daily on foot and on horseback from across the surrounding fields and the hills.

Consolidation left only ghosts of the schools she attended in Clear Spring and in Houston. And it left its mark on her restaurant.

"I don't mind now," she said with a degree of resignation. "I'm getting too slow for this business. I'm not that old, I guess. Just a lot of mileage. A restaurant will put the miles on you."

Some easier miles had been coming to her from a part-time job she held — driving a U.S. mail route. From Freetown to Norman Station, to Kurtz and to Courtland, and finally to Seymour, she put the miles on at the rate of fifty a day.

"It gives me a chance to go to the grocery store to buy what I need for the restaurant," she said of her excuse for holding a second job. "It's worth doing for that reason."

Her brother Larry Weekly was her employer. He drove the same route in the morning, delivering mail to the same communities from Seymour.

"He treats me fine," she said of working for him. "I start out at four o'clock in the afternoon and I come home when I want. One winter I got home a lot later than I wanted. It took me three hours to get over Hendershot Hill."

Reva's was a tiny place set right in the heart of Freetown. At one time sixty patrons could be seated in its single dining room. But those days were gone, and Reva had adjusted the seating capacity to about thirty.

"I'm not sure about the future of this place as a restaurant," Reva said with indecision. "I've been thinking about antiques; you know, dishes and pottery? I don't know."

I surveyed again the lady who had prepared the chicken lying thick and tender amid large yellow noodles on the plate before me, the mashed potatoes smothered in gravy and the garden peas.

"Antiques?" I groaned. "You can't mean it, Reva?"

Time, not antiques, eventually changed the face of Reva's place. To the casual passerby in Freetown there is no indication now that the homey little restaurant ever existed.

"THE ACTION PEOPLE"

There was a lived-in charm about the place that gave rise to a sense of welcome, a come-on-in-friend feeling. So it was not unusual that a preacher man's footsteps should have been directed to the old Kinder place on Route 1, Bloomfield, to ask if he might baptize six children in one of the two small lakes there.

So, early in October, Reverend Jon Chastain of the Allen's Chapel Methodist Church arrived, and he was welcomed with his baptismal candidates, their families, and a churchly entourage. And when the ceremony was finished Gary Cook, Kent Cook, Kim Cook, Cavin Cook, Karen Stalcup and Mark Norris had been taken wet and jubilant into the fold.

The event left Willard and Amanda Tilford, the residents of the old house, pleased and moved. They recorded it on color film.

"I was a little surprised that someone should want to use our lake like that," Willard said as they showed me the photos during my visit with them in the living room of the old house.

"Amanda was, too," he said. "We never thought of anything like that happening here. But we were glad to have them."

The Tilford modesty seemed as old fashioned as the old house. And like the old house it left a pleasingly genuine inpression on a visiting reporter.

The impression was strengthened when Willard said — and Amanda nodded in agreement — that he sometimes felt guilty over their good fortune, which included life, health, the proximity of nature, grown children, small grandchildren, and a great grandchild; and when he added that, "I've received blessings clean out of proportion with what I feel I've earned."

"Oh my goodness!"

That's how Norman Nierste began recounting what might be one of the reasons for Willard's and Amanda's blessings.

Nierste was the administrator of the Bloomfield Nursing Center, which was situated on North Seminary Street.

"They," Nierste continued speaking of the Tilfords, "have given us more than six thousand hours of their time in the last few years — something not many people would do. It is almost impossible to say enough for them."

Nierste was correct. It was almost impossible for anyone to say enough about the Tilfords. But I'm going to try — briefly.

Willard spent enough time in the Army, Navy, and at Crane to give him an early retirement. Amanda spent almost a quarter century at RCA in Bloomington before she decided to relax.

"We wanted to retire as early in life as possible," said Willard, "so that we might enjoy doing the things we most wanted to do, which includes the enjoyment of rural life and to be of help to others about us who were less fortunate than we."

The old Kinder place which Willard had purchased in 1941 was made up of twenty-five acres. Flattened out, as Willard said, it might have been one hundred acres. In addition to the two lakes of fish, it also abounded in cattle, chickens, peacocks, guineas, ducks, apples, peaches, plums, cherries, bees, fresh milk and maple syrup.

They had arrived at the Kinder place via two marriages — one for Willard, the other for Amanda — each of which was terminated by a tragic accident.

They met for the second time at a Crabbe School reunion in 1961. The first time was in the fifth grade

Willard and Amanda Tilford

at that school in 1926. And when they were married in 1965 and she came to live at the old Kinder place, she was teaching a Sunday School class at Owensburg Baptist Church and Willard was teaching one at Bloomfield Baptist Church.

He had a son, she had a son and a daughter. They all had children. One also had a grandchild, making Willard and Amanda great grandparents. They all joined them on the old Kinder place as often as possible, along with the plums and the peacocks and the cherries and the bees – and all. There also was a basketball court there, and Willard played there with his grandchildren every time they showed up.

Willard won many trophies as a speechmaker in Toastmasters. He had ridden a unicycle while dribbling a basketball and pushing a hoop and roller in area parades for many years — namely parades in Owensburg, Springville, Linton, Odon, and in Litchfield, Kentucky.

Amanda tended hundreds of flowers that grew on

the old Kinder place. She gardened and canned and cleaned, and was proud that "we live in our house," the love for which was contained in the warm summation that it was "too good a building to tear down and not hardly good enough to live in."

A wood heater, put into use after increases in the cost of heating fuel drove them to it, burned wood from the acres of timber on the old place. A chain saw and a buzz saw were used to obtain and prepare it for its ultimate use.

They had retained their membership in the Owensburg Baptist Church but the high cost of gasoline and oil had forced them to seek spiritual comfort in the nearby Tulip Baptist Church.

"Gasoline got so high," Amanda said. "Tulip Baptist is close enough to walk if we don't have any."

Somewhere in all this activity of life, Willard and Amanda had elevated to greater importance their contribution to those less fortunate than they.

"They come here every Monday and every Friday," Nierste said from the nursing home. "And they are here on the last Saturday of every month."

The Tilfords conducted bowling on Mondays — in a long hallway, or corridor, with heavy plastic pins and balls. They presented winners with prizes and beautiful trophies.

On Fridays they conducted Bible study, and Nierste said they had the residents of the home doing Bible lessons every week.

And on the last Saturday of the month they provided the men and women of the nursing facility with a birthday party at which all those who reached anniversaries the previous days of the month were honored.

Nierste said there were fifty-nine residents in the home and that their average age was about seventy-eight. He said they enjoyed the Tilfords and what the couple did for them.

"And," Nierste said, "the Tilfords sell cider at the Apple Festival every year in Bloomfield and give all the proceeds to the nursing home."

And he also said that the Tilfords "bring ducklings to show these people who are farm people, and ginseng and berries and bittersweet and all kinds of flowers."

"They are always available, always donating," he said.

"They just don't quit. We call them the 'Action People.' They are two wonderful people."

So it was not unusual that a preacher man should have stopped at the old Kinder place to ask if he might conduct a baptism there. The place exudes a notice-able charm that is Willard and Amanda Tilford.

ABANDONED

The wind is restless here on this deserted knoll, always in motion, moving, like the murky waters of the river below.

It sweeps up the lofty stone bluff cool and damp, and murmurs in the heights of sycamore, oak and poplar, then down again to whisper over ageless fields; tirelessly, relentlessly, in consuming loneliness.

Like an ethereal monument its ceaseless, whispery movement recounts a distressing change of fortune; a romance laden with hope and love and ambition; and death and sorrow.

Here, under the grasses that grow lush and green in summer, are entombed the earthly remains of an historic village. And there, where now the plow furrows the aged wound of heartbreak, were arrayed the village streets. There — over there to the south, at the foot of the bluff — the ancient river that moistens the restive wind flowed then even as it now flows. And all around, almost as far as the eye could see, the beautiful country rolled and tumbled into valleys of seasonal carpets of breathtaking hues.

The village had blossomed on this knoll. Already the county seat, and inspired by a dream that it would one day become the state capital, it grew to six hundred souls in four short years. Businesses flourished, and employment was available in a number of shops, two tanyards and a carding mill. And it was the center of commerce for half a hundred miles around.

Its destiny assured, the village attracted professional men, merchants and homemakers in increasing numbers. Its contributions to commerce reached out to distant places, and flatboats laden with its products followed the river to New Orleans and the world markets beyond. Few dreams had swelled the hearts of men with prouder achievement, and there was the ultimate dream still to be realized.

At some point in this surging tide of good fortune, a nightmare appended itself to the illusion. Villagers were felled by a deadly malignancy; a fever from the river, they believed, wafted up on the restless wind.

Medicines of the period were powerless in its path. The nightmare soon outgrew the noble dream, and the graveyard outpaced the growing village. As the disease continued its fatal spread, new settlers, merchants, and circuit riding judges and lawyers avoided the plagued village.

Death stalked this knoll with unyielding fury until too late the people learned that contaminated village wells, sunk into an extensive graveyard of Indian Mound Builders, was the real enemy. A sympathetic state legislature granted the dispirited people the right to move their village, their county seat; to relocate. Within seven years from the date of its inception, the dream lay shattered.

Embittered by disappointment and the awful death toll, the people of the village turned their despair against one another. A feud, whose echoes may still be heard, arose over the selection of a new village site; a new county seat; north or south of the murky waters of the river? After long and caustic argument, the village was moved north of the river, and its name was changed from Palestine to Bedford.

The exodus of all but about one third of the people from the stricken village was immediate. In fear of the deadly fever, some packed only their personal belongings, deserting the place as quickly as possible. Others moved their homes log by log, stone by stone, and reset them on the new site. Those who stayed, those who tried desperately to retain some remnant of the dream, slowly, sorrowfully, in the months to come, acquiesced. The unfortunate dead also were not left behind; they were disinterred and given a new place of rest in Green Hill Cemetery in the new county seat.

After ten years, the glorious hope had faded into the mists that rise up from the waters of the river below Palestine. And in the ensuing decades, the paraphernalia of life and living left behind returned to the earth from which it had come, and the restless wind whispered — still whispers — a haunting requiem to the passing.

Here, where the grasses grow lush and green in summer, where the seeds of hope were sown and died, only an occasional visitor comes to relive the dream — there is the courthouse, and all around is the village. There are the people walking in the streets, working in the tanyard, the carding mill. And there, from the river, come the sounds of flatboats being loaded.

And always there is the wind, sweeping up from the cool waters of the river below the bluff, sighing deeply over lonely, deserted Palestine, first seat of Lawrence County govenment.

FORTY-SEVEN KIDS TWO TO A SEAT

You'd wonder how a man could keep order — let alone teach — with forty-seven kids jammed into one small room and sitting two to a seat.

Lloyd Anderson claimed those were the conditions at Hobbieville when he taught there. He added with a smile and shake of his head that he was able to teach successfully.

Two to a seat wasn't confined to one-room schools, however. Some of us can recall similar conditions in multi-room schools. That's how we managed to take home cooties, mange and the epizooty. Not to mention bawling complaints of having had to sit in the same seat with a "girl!"

Homer Sylvester, Carolyn Carmichael, Reuger Hudson and Leslie Foddrill were four of those kids at Hobbieville. There were a lot more whose names escaped Mr. Anderson. But in the period that he taught there, four or five kids a year would graduate from the eighth grade, proving, I suppose, that he was able to teach them something in spite of the crammed conditions.

Hobbieville may have been the only two-to-a-seat classroom in his teaching experience, but it wasn't the only one-room school. At age twenty he taught eight grades in the one-room school in Center Township in Greene County.

The old structure was situated between Stanford and the junction of State Road 45 and State Road 54. It was later converted to a dwelling, and, according to Mr. Anderson, Homer Melville lived there at this time, "And," Mr. Anderson remembered, "He went to school there when I taught there."

Homer Melville did indeed go to school there, as did his wife Louise, when her name was Sullivan. While

Mr. Anderson was teaching Homer at the fifth-grade level, he was teaching Louise at the first. Two other Sullivan girls and one boy also attended that school, according to Louise: Mildred, Imogene, and Kenneth. That's not all. Charlotta (Lottie) Combs Sullivan, their mother, also attended that school.

In 1958 the Melvilles converted the old school building into a home for themselves and their two sons, and, as Mr. Anderson said, they were still living there at this time.

"The little kids used to sit right here," Homer indicated the living room of the home when I visited them. "And right there," he pointed toward the kitchen, "is where the big kids sat."

The entire eight grades faced north, and lessons usually appeared on a wide poplar board at that end of the building.

Homer and Louise had determined from their land abstract that the building may have been built around 1892.

In the more than thirty-one years that Mr. Anderson taught school he was assigned and reassigned at various times to Sandborn, Hobbieville, Bodwell, Cincinnati, Solsberry and Owensburg in Greene County; and at Clay, Thrasher and Chapel Hill schools in Monroe County.

Hired and assigned by township trustees, he earned an annual wage of eight hundred dollars. One year the township couldn't meet its obligations and Mr. Anderson settled for fifty dollars less than that amount.

"We raised our family on eight hundred dollars a year," Mr. Anderson said of his and Irene Anderson's lifetime effort. "Of course," Mr. Anderson pointed out, "I worked every summer vacation in order for us to be able to do that."

Meaning understood.

Most teachers of his time also farmed or pursued other means of earning money in addition to teaching to supplement their eight hundred dollar salaries in order to pay their year's expenses.

The Andersons reared six children: Jim, Joan, Joseph, Janice, Richard and Carolyn. At this time they were looking forward to their forty-eighth wedding anniversary.

Had his hearing not failed him slightly, Mr. Anderson would have continued teaching.

"But," he recalled his decision to quit, "I'd hear a noise I thought came from one direction and come to find out it came from another."

Although embarrassing in some ways, the impairment must have been slight. Mr. Anderson went from teaching to a job at Indiana University, his alma mater. Later he took a job with General Electric. In neither case did his hearing interfere with his ability to do the job.

Looking back on the school years, Mr. Anderson recalled that the "last day dinners" were far and away the best of the better events to come into a school teacher's life.

"The whole neighborhood would turn out," he said. "They'd bring good food, talk about the school year and pat you on the back for doing a good job.

"They quit doing that sort of thing, and they've stopped locking the teacher out at Christmas time," he said. "The lockouts were for treats — the kids wanted treats from their teachers. If the teacher didn't promise to bring them treats, they'd lock him or her out of school."

Once, while teaching at Thrasher School, a little boy fell and injured his leg. Believing it may have been serious, Mr. Anderson made numerous offers to see the child home. The boy refused each time, saying he was all right. However, on the way home that afternoon he collapsed. He was later found by his worried, searching parents.

"His father came to school the next day and told me that it was broken," Mr. Anderson said. "He knew about me trying to get the little boy to let me take him home, and he wasn't angry. He just wanted me to know.

"I think about that every so often," he said. "You see, I let that little fellow talk me out of taking him home. Not once, but several times."

When we talked, Mr. Anderson was retired and living at R. 1, Solsberry. He walked daily, and when the season was in he gardened.

"I like to garden," he said. "And I always loved children."

Which probably explained why he was able to teach forty-seven kids jammed two to a seat in a one-room school.

A STORY OF HOPE

As the yellow Olds station wagon raced northward on I-465 near Indianapolis, the driver reviewed his plan. It was simple. He had seen the huge abutment many times in his travels as a salesman. An image of it appeared in his mind. He saw it again, clearly, at the 71st Street Exit. It appeared sufficiently large enough to serve his need. Once there he would simply turn the steering wheel. The speeding car would crash head-on into the immovable concrete structure. And he, the driver, would be dead. It would be that simple.

Robert E. (Bob) O'Rourke had never before in his thirty-eight years been more certain of himself. He was going to commit suicide. Take his own life. Kill himself. And nothing could deter him. Nothing!

Satisfied with this final act he was to commit, O'Rourke, father of five, took one last look out the windows of the speeding station wagon. He was unmoved by what he saw out there. He'd seen it hundreds of times. He was not impressed. As he returned his eyes to the highway ahead something on the seat beside him caught his eye. It was a pint of whiskey.

"Mygod!"

Realization washed over O'Rourke like a shower of ice water.

"If I hit that abutment," he shouted with ear-splitting clarity, "I'll break that bottle."

He jerked his foot off the accelerator. The speedometer needle dropped to 90. . . 80 . . . 60. The Olds passed the 71st Street abutment at a crawl. O'Rourke was going back home. Back to the life he had tried to escape. Back to the life of an alcoholic.

"I was drinking a fifth to a quart of whiskey every day, seven days a week," he told me during a visit with him and his wife, Chy. He hurried to add, "Not counting what I drank in taverns or in professional men's clubs, of course."

He kept supplies of whiskey in hiding places — in the station wagon's tire well, under the cushions of chairs and the davenport, in the toilet tank, under his mattress.

"I'd wake up in the middle of the night and I'd have to have a drink," he said of the last hiding place. "And before I could get out of bed I'd have to have one. And before I shaved."

O'Rourke began his affair with booze at the tender age of fifteen. Employed by a drinking boss who "sent me to the back door" of a tavern to obtain liquor which his employer left opened and in plain view, the boy began sneaking samples. He enjoyed the taste. He enjoyed the effect.

Because the cost of whiskey was more than he could afford in those early years, O'Rourke settled for beer. It wasn't as tasty as whiskey, nor was the effect exactly the same. But it would serve his purpose. He was not aware that his purpose was the beginning of an addiction. When he married at twenty-one he still was not aware of his problem.

Chy O'Rourke recalled the accepted and expected social life of that period.

"That was when we were jitterbugging and spiking Cokes," she said. "Everybody did it. I didn't suspect Bob had a problem. He didn't either."

It wasn't until a decade later that O'Rourke realized he was drinking abnormally. He didn't know why he was overindulging in booze. And he didn't want to know why. He was too content drinking.

His alcoholism began eating away at the fabric of family life. He hocked his spare tire to get enough money for a drink. He hocked just about everything he could get his hands on. On payday he'd reclaim his possessions.

He was forced by the dual needs of his family and the cost of his addiction to hold down two full time jobs: one as a buyer in a department store, the other as a bartender. He worked this way for almost five years until he became a traveling salesman for an auto parts firm. As a salesman, O'Rourke was able to earn enough on one job to support his family and his habit.

"There are two facts about alcoholics," he said of holding two jobs and his continued success as a salesman. "When they are drinking, when booze is available to them, they are the hardest workers you will ever find. They can out-produce most normal persons. And they are honest.

"But," he cautioned, "when they don't have money, they'll do anything for a drink. They'll lie, cheat and steal. And they can't work, and won't work."

His earnings as a salesman, however, were not enough to assuage his family's broken home life. He provided well for his wife and his children. But, he admits, his drinking was more important to him. It was more important than anything else in the whole world.

"I used to wait up for him," Chy remembered. "We had no peace of mind. I used to tell the children, 'Daddy didn't go to work today because he is sick,' or make some other excuse. But they got older, and they knew. Then they'd say things like, 'Mother, can you get him off to bed,' before their friends came over.

"At one of their Christmas parties he came in and I tried to steer him away from the children, and he fell. It was terribly embarrassing for the kids," she said.

There came a time when O'Rourke took to living in the basement of their expensive home. Whiskey and a radio were his only companions. When Sunday came, he ate his only meal of the week and he couldn't keep it down. Chy candidly remembered that episode in their lives.

"It was like having a creature in the basement," she said.

While she was at work one day, she was called to the telephone. It was her husband.

"I'm sick," he told her. "And I'm sick of being sick. I need help."

It was the moment Chy had been praying for, because only an alcoholic can make that decision for himself. She arranged to take some time off. She sped home. She helped her husband into her car and took him to an Alcoholics Anonymous center.

"Just get him to the door," she was told by a man who had answered the telephone call she'd made to AA before she left her job.

"When an alcoholic wants to go to the hospital," O'Rourke said, "get him there as fast as you can. Right then."

O'Rourke left the AA center two weeks later, dried out and determined to never drink again. A pal bet him $100 that he wouldn't last ninety days on the wagon. O'Rourke took the bet. At the end of the ninety-day dry spell, the pal paid off, and he and O'Rourke celebrated by drinking up the hundred dollars.

"After three months you'd think they'd be able to handle the craving," Chy said in recollection of that heartbreaking spree. "But they can't. It's always there."

She recalled the fears of those ninety days and nights; how she listened for her husband's footsteps from the car to the house. Were they steady? Unsteady? How she feared his announcement that he was going out to buy a pack of cigarettes. Or how she listened as her husband's car entered the driveway. Even from that sound she could determine if he was drunk or sober. She lived in dread of witnessing again familiar tricks, familiar sounds.

As the wife of an alcoholic during those years prior to her husband's brief dry spell, Chy, when he returned to the booze, found it easy to turn again to the children, to give her life to them.

"It was wrong. I know that now," she said. "There was Al-Anon, to help the wives of alcoholics, and Ala-Teen, for their families. We could have helped him had we gone to them. We could at least have coped sensibly with his problem."

O'Rourke continued drinking until Christmas Eve, 1969. On that night he came up from his hermitage in the basement and handed Chy a gaily wrapped package. Inside she found an empty whiskey bottle. He had drunk its contents before wrapping it.

"I hope," he said, "that this is the end." He was quick to add, "This is not a promise. I just hope."

Chy's eyes welled with tears at the memory.

"Every day," she said through a constricted throat, "was like a gift. We counted them. And we celebrated every week. We celebrated every month."

In later years they reserved their celebrations for the anniversary of O'Rourke's accomplishment — Christmas Eve.

"I never dreamed," Chy said of those frightful years, "that we'd ever get to this place."

"This place" was a combination of three profitable businesses. All three were situated next door to a tavern. It was in "this place" that I visited with the O'Rourkes to obtain this account of his battle with the bottle. Why did they tell me?

"Hope," said Chy. "This is a story of hope for every alcoholic and his or her family who reads it. If it can be of help to one of them — and there are so many of them — the story of Bob's alcoholism and his victory over it will be worthwhile. There is no shame in it. There is no shame in being an alcoholic and to ask for help."

"All this," O'Rourke added raising his arms to the businesses around us, "is available to anyone who quits — if they want it badly enough."

THE CAT-SKINNER

You've probably wondered all your life if that old saw about there being more than one way to skin a cat can possibly be true. Well, it is, and Clifford P. (Red) Banta would have been just the man to have proved it to you.

Of course, you'd have got your shoe-shine dusty, and even muddy, for a close-up view of him proving it, and you'd have felt your heart in your throat when he teetered the big cat on the edge of a high embankment, but your curiosity would have been forever satisfied.

Red, who with his wife Beulah lived at Ketcham Road and Victor Pike in Monroe County, had been skinning a variety of cats since the early 1940s, when he climbed aboard his first cat as a Seabee.

"They taught me how," he told me on the job one day during a cigarette break. "I wanted to join the Navy, but they told me I was color blind. They'd flash them colors right quick and say, 'Name them off.' Then they said, 'You're color blind.' And I said, 'Awww, I'm not color blind. Baloney.'"

Ten days after his boot camp leave the Navy shipped Red off to the South Pacific, along with the 77th Seabees, and his "color blind" eyes.

It was "hot" where they sent him, Red said. A place called Guadalcanal, "where you couldn't lay a hand down on the beach without it'd touch a maggot, there were so many dead U.S. servicemen there."

He "skun" those cats on the Canal, building airstrips, roads and emplacements, and then moved on to Vella Lavella, and on to Bougainville, and to the Bismarck Archipelago, with two Marines riding shotgun on the seat beside him to protect him from Japanese snipers. That was the only way to get the job done.

"We had twenty-seven months of it right on arunnin'," Red said, remembering those months of that long ago Pacific war with a shake of his head. "Then we went to Australia for a rest."

The 77th also was sent to Australia to rebuild itself, for it was torn to shreds by the Japanese.

Standing in the sun and the dust talking to Red you'd have found it hard to place him on one of those PD-14 International cats, getting shot at. He was smiley, freckled, red-haired, easy-going, and his voice was a soft, disarming rasp.

But he'd been there. Building those strips, those roads. And building beaches for the Marines to land on. All of which was known back here then as the Road to Tokyo.

LSTs were knocked out from under his 77th, and cats were blasted into the bloody seas with the 77th's dead, but a remnant survived, and one of that fortunate group was Red.

When U.S. planes fell, or were shot down into the jungles of those islands, they called on the cat-skinners to rescue their pilots. Red made his share of trips into those jungles, often at night.

"I remember one night," he recounted one such experience, "that a cat died on us. We had to leave it and start back on foot. Along about daylight a brush hen flushed up in front of us with a big who-o-o-sh. Boy, I'll tell you we thought we'd had it."

Cat-skinners in the Navy construction battalions (SEABEES) worked four hours and were off four hours, twenty-four hours a day. "When those fellers'd start putting holes in our tanks and our radiators," Red said of being under fire, "we'd bail off them things, and the Marines would shoot back. Got one, one day, too. He was up in a coconut tree."

The 77th joined the legendary First Marine Division on the Canal, and at Bougainville they linked up with the Third Division.

"The Navy took us there," Red recalled that night-time landing on Bougainville. "Then they went off and left us. The next thing we knowed, ships was blinking lights at us while we was trucking supplies back up in the hills.

"Then all of a sudden here comes these big U.S. Navy battlewagons, and we could see them in the night, and they was coming full speed ahead, and was going to blow us off that island.

"Two-thirds of us didn't know what the blinking meant nohow, and finally we started blinking the truck lights back at them, and that settled them down. Boy, I'll tell you, that was close."

After resting and rebuilding itself in Australia, Red's outfit shipped out for the Philippines where, he said, during and after its landing, it took another twenty-seven months of hell in one day.

"Takes you years and years t'get over a thing like that," Red said. "Even now, at night in bed — why when you hear a plane sometimes it all comes back, and you're going to get under that bed."

And when he was cat-skinning in perfect safety, many years later, he'd sometimes "get the feeling that I'm going to get it."

Red attempted to smile his way out of answering specific questions, or he'd say, "Awww, it wasn't nothin'." But I had to know his worst World War II experience with the 77th, and I hung in there until he told me.

"I guess you'd say making the graveyards," he said. Graveyards?

"Yeah, on Vella Lavella, especially," he continued. "We just dug a big hole with our cats, and then we pushed our fellers into it, just like you would cord-wood. They was stacked around like cord-wood."

Nineteen years after the war was over the Navy

caught up with Red and presented him with four Bronze Stars and a Silver Star.

"It was 1964," he smiled. "Them four bronze ones was for four major battles, and I don't know what the silver one was for. And all of them other medals I got I don't know neither. Bunch of fruit salad (a reference to the colorful uniform campaign ribbons that represent the medals)."

Curious, I asked Red if one of them might be a Purple Heart. He took a last drag on the cigarette and smiled.

"Awww," he said running his fingers through his curly red hair, "I didn't get no Purple Heart. I was always a-runnin' too fast."

He saluted me and tossed the cigarette butt — he saluted everyone — and climbed back up on the big 955L Caterpillar. The diesel sputtered then roared. Red, who was employed by C. E. Crider and Son, Lampkins Ridge, in Bloomington, continued skinning the Cat on a familiar job, building a new graveyard — for the dead who hopefully will not have to be buried like cordwood.

BESSIE BURCH

Sunday school teacher Lena Alexander, Walter's wife, had assigned her three verses from 1 Corinthians, Chapter 13, to recite for the Mothers Day program, and thirteen year old Bessie Burch was worried.

She was not alone in her concern. Eva Ellis, Jessie Thrasher and Etta Weaver also had verses from Chapter 13 to recite and they were also anxious. But Bessie Burch's trepidation came not from fear, for she had studied and rehearsed Verses 11, 12, and 13, and knew them well. So well had she learned them that even many years later, at age ninety-eight, she still remembered them.

No, her anxiety came from embarrassment rather than fright. Her only pair of shoes were so old and worn they had holes on the sides and the little toe on each foot stuck out. And she was determined not to appear like that before the whole church.

"I couldn't get up and say a piece with ragged shoes like that on and my toes sticking out," she remembered one morning when I visited with her. "I had an older pair of shoes and I cut pieces out of them and sewed them over the holes."

The patches improved the looks of the shoes, but they still were quite obviously old and beaten. Turning over a lid on the wood range before starting out for church that Sunday morning she daubed a wet rag into the soot and creosote there, and blackened the shoes, especially the patches she had sewn on them. On the three-mile hike to church she had to wade Beech Creek. Rather than damage her newly repaired and blackened shoes, she took them off and forded the creek barefoot.

"Oh," she sucked in her breath with a gasp at the memory, "the water was cold. When I got across the creek I put my shoes back on and went on to church."

The occasion was not only Mothers Day, it was the first Mothers Day to be celebrated at the Solsberry Methodist Church. The date was May 10, 1910. Attired in a new rose-pattern dress she had made herself and standing in her patched and blackened shoes, Bessie recited her three verses, beginning with the verse that reads: "When I was a child I spoke as a child . . ." without making a mistake.

Bessie and I met while she was in the midst of a five day visit at the one hundred-seventy acre farm of her daughter Joann Jacob and her husband, Joseph, on Wright Road, in Greene County. A native of the Solsberry area, Bessie's home at this time was in Arthur, Ill., where she'd been living alone in a small two-bedroom house since the loss of her husband Rollie. Despite her advanced age, she still was able to read her Bible and the newspaper, and she still did her own sewing.

When she was a child her mother, Sarah, daily saw her off on the mile walk to classes at the same one-room Sandborn School her father, Frank Gardner, had attended.

"We used to pray and sing a religious song in class every day," she recalled her school days. "We made our own flag. Our teacher, Grace Glover, one of the best teachers who ever went in a school room, got the material, and we cut out the stars and stripes. She sewed them for us on her sewing machine; a great big flag. The boys put up a big flag pole and we pledged allegiance to that flag every morning that it went up."

There were eight grades in the single schoolroom and Bessie worked her way through all of them, graduating after completing the eighth. She continued living in the Solsberry area until she was seventeen. Then she and Rollie eloped; they got on one of four

Illinois Central passenger trains that daily choo-chooed through Solsberry and rode it to Effingham, Ill. There they bought a marriage license and found a judge who married them. They spent the next month at the home of Rollie's brother in Humboldt.

Back in Indiana, Rollie had breathing problems that seemed to be aggravated by the weather. They left Indiana in 1928 for what they expected to be a permanent home in Illinois. They had nine children. Three of them, Ralph, Lonnie and Dale, who served in the Army during World War II, were all overseas at the same time. One of them, Ralph, was in combat for eleven months. It was painful for Bessie and Rollie, but they knew that they were only two of many parents throughout the U.S. who had two or more sons in service in that war at the same time. There were no such things as support groups for them to turn to. No counselors. They did what Bessie and Rollie did.

"I worked in a war plant and we prayed and asked the Lord to care for our sons and to get them home safe," she said.

Bessie also wrote letters to her sons, and they wrote back. One, a V-Mail letter she remembered, was written by her son Ralph while he crouched in a foxhole. It was hardly legible. "I have no pencil," it read, "so I am writing this with a bullet. I'm okay and I hope I stay this way."

All her sons survived the war. When she questioned one of them about a bronze star he'd been awarded, he told a strange story. He recounted a battle in which many men on both sides had fallen mortally wounded. One, a young enemy soldier, was gravely hurt but still alive.

"I carried him piggy-back to our side where he got help," he told his mother.

Bessie had many more wonderful memories that

her children never tired of hearing. She had a hundred and twenty-six of them: children, grandchildren, great grandchildren and great great grandchildren. And she loved to come to Indiana to visit, flying some of the time, this time making the hundred and fifty mile trip to Greene County by automobile.

Bessie Burch

THE BELL

They took Sallie Sargent home to Burns City the other day. The trip had been scheduled for an earlier date but had to be postponed because of the winter's biggest snowfall. And since there is always a loss of attendance if an interment doesn't immediately follow a requiem, it was a lonely sort of journey. And, too, most of her friends had preceded her there, as had her husband, John Taylor Sargent.

Familiar names abounded on the surrounding stone markers in the cemetery across from Sallie's old church: Keck, Winkelpeck, Osborn, Wikel, Langford, Webster, Kutch, Summerville, Sims, McNabb, Vickers, Holt, Garrett, Toon, and so many others.

In their lifetimes, some had attended school with Sallie when as a child she rode horseback to the community's single classroom. Later, as a woman among the women of her time there, she was visited by Dr. Thomas Alvin Hayes who arrived at her house on horseback, or by roadcart or buggy, to deliver her nine children.

They were a special kind of people, Sallie and her friends. Most were born and reared in primitive homes, usually constructed of logs and equipped with few or no conveniences. And in the Holt School where they learned to read and write and do arithmetic, they drank from the same dipper that hung by a single bucket of well water.

It was an unhealthy practice. Yet the majority of them lived long, productive lives. Sallie, had she lived a little longer, would have been ninety-nine on her next birthday, June 30.

Recalling those early days at Burns City, Sallie, almost two years earlier, on the eve of her ninety-seventh birthday told me, "We got around on horseback.

118

We went to school that way — and to church, and to Sunday School.

"We got around on horseback when it snowed, too. But we didn't have much going to do, when it snowed, like people do now," she said. She expressed the reason in these words: "We didn't have much buying to do except if we ran out of coffee, sugar, rice or salt."

The church Sallie rode to on horseback was the Christian Church. It had stood abandoned there in Burns City for years. At the time of Sallie's death, the once white exterior clapboard walls had turned gray, and were blistered and dirty. Tall window openings were sealed from the elements with lengths of metal corrugated roofing.

The ground around the old structure was covered with wild growth. The intact pipe-banistered concrete stairway up which so many climbed from the road in front of the building to reach a place of worship led to a derelict hulk.

The church was a victim of the times, as were so many churches in small-town U.S.A. War, better jobs and greater mobility scattered their flocks. Cast off, "God's houses" withered and died.

When carpenter John Taylor Sargent took a job away from Burns City, Sallie and their family went with him. But she retained an attachment for the place where she was born and reared.

"I was born there in 1881," she had informed me. "I went to Sunday school and church there; I graduated from common school there in 1897; I was married there in 1898; all my children were born there; my husband is buried there. How could I forget it?" she said.

It was this strong sentiment that aroused her fears for the bell that hung in the belfry of the abandoned church.

"It belongs to the people who paid for it," she said. "I was still a girl yet when Becky Holt went walking around from house to house taking up donations to buy it. And most of those who gave are now buried in the cemetery across the road.

"If that belfry rots down," she said fearfully, "someone is going to steal the bell and take it away and get a lot of money for it. I want to see it taken down and put in concrete on a high place in the cemetery. But wherever it would be set there, I'd be happy about it. I'd even give to help pay for the moving of it," she said.

When they took Sallie home to Burns City the other day, the bell was not there. Across the road from her resting place, the belfry atop her abandoned church stood gaping to the east and south — those walls removed — and its interior yawned shadowed and empty.

After Sallie had made her desire known, John Sargent, her grandson, and his friend, Mike Clark, both of Spencer, climbed to the church roof, removed the two belfry walls, dismantled the pulley from the bell, and lowered the separate parts by rope to the ground. On the ground they were aided by Don Sargent, Sallie's son and John's father, Floyd Wade, from R. 2, Odon, and Ed Witsman, Burns City, who now owned the building and the ground.

Sallie was aware of the bell's removal from the church to her son's home in Spencer, and that dispelled her fears for its loss. Although it had not yet been installed in the cemetery when they took her home the other day, it is there now.

BROMER

Robert Hoggart shook his head.

"By guineas," he exclaimed, "they're about all gone."

Bromer's old timers were about all gone, and few there were, if any, who made up its population of thirty-three souls, who had seen the Bromer of old, the Bromer that was there before it slipped into legend.

"I wasn't here," Hoggart said, puffing on a Swisher Sweet Cigar. "But I heered Roy Corn'ell tell about it."

Dropping the "W" in Cornwell seemed a common and accepted practice among the older folks in and around Bromer. They also had their own pronunciation of the name of the nearby community of Syria. The final vowel was given the sound of "E" and the "Y" was pronounced so that the name Syria came out "s-o-r-r-y."

Hoggart could have been sixty-five, or he could have been seventy-five, he would not say. He looked either age. He labored pretty much as a younger man would have, caring for seven hundred laying Bob White Quail, two thousand five-hundred chicks he was readying for sale, incubators full of quail eggs, thirteen pointer dogs he was training for sale, and two beagle hounds.

He was a late-comer to Bromer, having arrived from Bono in Lawrence County some three or four decades before 1975. His arrival was in time to purchase the old Henry Stratton General Store that won notoriety before the turn of the century when it was moved from the west to the east side of State Road 237.

"It was moved and they never shut the doors, just kept doing business all the time," Hoggart said.

Hoggart operated the general store in Bromer until the advent of the modern supermarket in nearby towns and cities. Six stalwart Amish men later razed the old store building for him one day in appreciation for past favors, and Hoggart used the lumber to reconstruct a huge birdhouse over the store's original location.

He had arrived in Bromer in time to also buy Clark E. Doak's blacksmith shop, and he operated that, he said, "Until I sharpened a million plow points on the forge."

It was while the building resounded to Doak's old singing anvil under Hoggart's hammer that Hoggart made his several friendships among the Amish around Bromer.

Although he had its rack of boxes in a woodworking shop flanking the other side of the bird house, opposite the blacksmith shop, Hoggart did not remember the Bromer post office. Neither did Courtney Boone who spent his childhood and adolescent years in the small Orange County community.

Seated in a lawn chair in his brother Carmen's maple-shaded, breezy yard Courtney remembered his father's recollections of early Bromer.

"There was a general store here, a cream station, a barber shop, and an ice house," he said.

He recalled, too, that in the house where the Obert Whalens lived, a remodeled white frame, a milliner had a shop.

From behind the counter of the Easterday Brothers Grain Co. where she worked at the time, Jean Boone said of the milliner, "Minnie Trabune was her name."

Phil, Dan, and Tom were the Easterdays, a successful trio of brothers who also owned Easterday Implements, where John Deere products were sold.

In the distance around Bromer the rolling hills of southern Indiana rose on a hazy horizon. But Bromer, and the thousands of acres lying between it and the hills were comparatively flat. They were green and tall in corn with bronze, tasseled tops.

"There was no glacial action here," Courtney, a former mayor of Boca Raton, Florida, said of a horse-shoe-shaped flat that ran northward from Rockport in the southwest, to Martinsville in the north, and down to New Albany in the southeast.

Easterday's served farmers in a seven or eight mile radius who averaged one hundred bushels of corn to the acre, and about thirty-five bushels of beans on farms ranging in size from twenty acres to a thousand acres. Their granery, at year's end, was expected to open to some seven hundred tons of that grain. A St. Louis-based wire service in the Easterday office tick-ticked constantly as it reported market prices from almost every area of the U.S.

Grazing draft horses appeared on Amish farms around Bromer, and the jiggle and jounce of Amish buggies were as some ghostly sound out of its ancient past, or at least in startling contrast to the grind and roar of the huge trucks entering and exiting the busy Easterday granery. Courtney Boone remembered a time when wagons and buggies were in vogue, and they were just about the only transportation out of Bromer to Orleans to the northwest, from Bromer to Syria to the west, Millersburg to the south, Livonia — they pronounced it lye-von-yah — to the southeast, and Salem to the east.

Courtney completed eight grades in the Bromer one-room school before going to high school in Orleans. He graduated from there in 1927. After the school building was abandoned it became a part of the Easterday granery.

Hoggart remembered, "Roy Con'ell a-tellin' it, that farmers used to drive their flocks of turkeys into Bromer."

They were butchered and dressed behind the old general store and shipped to surrounding markets.

"There was a Bromer church here, too, back then," said Hoggart. "But I never did hear what the nationality was."

THE FIDDLER

From Goose Bay to Alaska, from Washington, D. C. to California, at points in and out of the USA, the name Jimmy Campbell is remembered with pleasure and affection.

The man, Jimmy Campbell, lived at the end of a long lane of Mel Currie Road, west of the Dolan Flats. He was a fiddler of old time tunes and it was this talent that endeared him to many students from near and far who studied at the Indiana University Folklore Institute in Bloomington.

Jimmy was sixty-six years old when we met. Gray of hair, blue of eye and bespectacled, he pinched Velvet pipe tobacco from a leather pouch into yellow wheat straw paper which he rolled into a neat smoke, ultimately to hang smoking from a far corner of his mouth.

"There's no taste to the paper, and when you roll your own you don't smoke so much," Jimmy explained his preference for the roll-your-own over tailor-made cigarettes.

He had been a favorite of folklorists for twenty years, and not entirely because of his music. Jimmy's family went back to County Antrim, Ireland. His great-great grandfather settled near Bloomington after the Civil War, in which he had participated as a member of Co. F, 27th Indiana Regulars.

According to Jimmy, the elder Campbell had fought at Winchester, Cedar Mountain, was wounded at Antietam, was back in action for the fight at Chancellorsville, was wounded at Gettysburg, and in the fight at Resaca he fractured an arm.

Jimmy remembered tales from early days: how, for example, folks used to walk from the Dolan area to church services on North Walnut Street in Bloomington every Sunday.

"They'd walk barefoot to Griffey Creek where they'd wash their feet, then put on their socks and shoes and go on to church," he said, and he smiled at his own conjuring up of that sight from an imagination whose embers were easily inflamed.

Jimmy had long, vertical creases on each side of his square jaw and a smile would pull them awry, etching into his face a reposing warmness which was further lulled by the easy drowsiness of his words.

When I arrived at the Campbell home, unannounced, Jimmy and his wife, Eula, dropped everything and we retired to a long concrete block building with a green-shingled gambrel roof. In one small room of that building where a collection of watches and clocks covered the walls, and banjoes in and out of cases, and fiddles in their cases were at rest on tables, or lounging against the lower part of the walls, we eased ourselves into creaky old chairs.

"This is a boar's nest," Jimmy apologized for the appearance of the place as he began the construction of another cigarette. A watch and clock repairman, Jimmy had spent countless hours in the room. Although he detailed in his drowsy way how he learned watchmaking while confined to a bed for six long years with an illness that had left him with a limp, I got the feeling that his happiest hours in the room were not given to his vocation. They were those hours he shared with other fiddlers, other musicians, for his voice and his eyes brightened so at the recollection of the many sessions held there.

Music came into his life at an early age via the jew's harp and, later, a French harp. He recalled many music schools in the Bloomington area, and how well attended they were. "Used to be that almost anyone could pick up a strange song and sing it right out by note," he said at one point.

Photographic memories were also a part of a visit with Jimmy and, from the many he showed me, he lingered longest over one of the Bloomington Hoosier Charm Band, whose members included Ed Gourley, David Johnson, John Marlin, Joseph Marlin, Norman Johnston, McClellan Taurner, William Brown, William Wood, William Griffith, Bert Farmer and Freeland Larue.

And another group with whom he also had played: Chester Frame, Maurice and Bob Hardy. They called themselves the Hoosier Vagabonds. And there were others, like Shorty Hagan and John Fleenor.

Square dances — the old fashion kind — were, Jimmy's forte. "Didn't matter how cold it got or how icy," Eula noted, "We went all over." Jimmy even then was scheduled to fiddle for a square dance at Virgil Fulford's east of Hindustan.

"Music is a relaxing sort of thing," Jimmy observed. "I'd work a twelve-hour day and come home plumb give out, and a bunch would come over and get a session started out here and in a little bit I'd be relaxed and feel good again."

The "bunch" came over every Wednesday evening, and anybody was invited, with or without a musical instrument.

"I've wished many, many times that I had kept a register," Jimmy said of the visits and music sessions with the IU folklorists of the previous twenty years. "They came from all over the country, all over the world to hear me play the fiddle and to play their instruments along with me. Ah, they're a good bunch. Some of those kids are really something."

As he played the "Peacock Rag" for me his right foot loudly smacked the floor. And then he said, "Rags are a little peculiar. This one starts off in G and goes off into E, A, D, and then back to G." And then he was off and into "Hell on Buck Creek," "Soldier's Joy," and "Buffalo Nickel." All for me.

"A grad student at the university plays violin. He said he'd like to learn to play by ear," Jimmy recounted the desire of one student who visited the little room in the long concrete block building. "I suspect he'll have a lot of trouble. He'll have to forget what he knows and learn all over," he said.

Fiddling didn't come as easy for Jimmy as it had for some.

"I had to work a long time to get out a lick," he said. "There's a lot in (how you handle) your bow."

Jimmy held the fiddle to his chest when he played it, and he would halt the sawing of the bow over the strings now and then to speak to me.

"A feller asked an old time fiddler once if he knew any music," Jimmy smiled, "and the old boy said, 'Well, I don't know enough to hurt my playing it.'"

THE WISDOM OF JOE

While eating spaghetti and meatballs at a Bloomington restaurant one evening I suddenly put down my plastic tableware, took a ballpoint and a three-by-five file card from my shirt pocket, and began making notes.

"What are you writing?" my wife, who was eating vermicelli alfredo with broccoli, wanted to know.

Something had reminded me of an old friend and I wanted to record my thoughts as quickly as possible before they slipped away. But my answer to her was much briefer than that. "Column," I said. "Just be a minute."

The short lengths of spaghetti I had been hopelessly trying to twirl Italian style on a small plastic fork with the aid of a small plastic spoon had called to mind a man whom scores of people in his long lifetime had known only as Joe.

An Italian immigrant, he was a dry cleaner who operated stores which at different times occupied three separate downtown Bedford locations. Although his business was named "Bedford Cleaning Works," most people referred to it simply as "Joe's" or "Joe's Place."

It mattered little to Joe what people called it, the flow of dollars was steady and that was of much pride and a great deal of satisfaction to him. If anything else might have mattered, it undoubtedly had to be the quality of his work. He took great pains in making it good.

He considered his work an art. A job well done pleased him immensely. There were no lingering odors after his cleaning, and the creases he pressed in trousers were always knife-like; never any double creases. There were other cleaners who did good work. Joe's was better than good.

He sought no praise. The customer expected a good job. He provided it. The customer paid for it. He appreciated it. It was business. And it was all accomplished without the waste of empty and soon forgotten words. His business philosophy was simple and pure. Give your best.

Joe came to the U.S. from the small town of Fuscaldo, Italy, in 1907, at age twenty-six. He brought with him an unmistakably Italian name: Giuseppi Siciliani. Because all Giuseppis who came to America sooner or later became Joes, he was not spared, and he already was Joe — Joe Siciliani — when he arrived in Bedford in 1913.

An experienced presser at the time, he worked in that capacity for a while at The Toggery, which, for many years, was an exclusive men's shop on Bedford's Courthouse Square.

After opening his own business, he devoted himself to it completely. To make it a success he worked from early morning until late at night, usually without supper, proud of every garment that passed through his hands.

Summer evenings and weekends he reserved for a bountiful vegetable garden, of which he was also proud. There he lovingly cared for tomatoes, peppers, string beans and other good things to eat, which grew in neat rows. The sheer beauty of those gardens down through the years once prompted a neighbor to respectfully observe, "Boy! Those eye-tal-yons. They can make things grow on solid rock."

Joe was fiercely proud of something else, and that was the fact that he was a naturalized citizen of the United States. For his entire lifetime he spoke of his citizenship as he might have spoken of some holy thing, he was so proud.

"The very best country in the world. A land of fine

people," he once told me during a visit. "But," he went on to say with a shake of his head, "they watch too much television." And he added, "Television is too silly."

Rather than watch television, he believed people needed more to speak with one another, to converse regularly on a variety of subjects, and to enjoy time together, communicating thoughts, opinions, ideas.

Joe had celebrated his ninety-sixth birthday the day before we'd had our visit. Although that was a long time ago I haven't forgotten him. Life's daily happenings have a way of stirring up memories, and often I am reminded of those who through the years have paraded through my many lines of type.

That is what happened when my wife and I were eating in a so-called Italian restaurant that evening. I was reminded of Joe and of something else he had said during our visit so long ago.

"I love this country," he intoned at one point, his chin moving up and down as though in agreement with what he was saying. "But there are a couple of things Americans just don't do very well."

Joe had a habit of pausing briefly between sentences and making a fine line of his mouth. While he was momentarily silent, I was patiently curious. When he was ready he spoke.

"One thing Americans don't do very well," he said, "is make wine."

His mouth again became a fine line, and when he again opened it he said, "The other is spaghetti."

CANCER

At a pitch-in gathering of older folks at Wilson Park, in Bedford, a certain balding gentleman appeared to be a shoe-in for a prize to the person having the least hair. But before he could open his mouth to claim it a spunky lady named Lorene Sallee took off the dinky little cap she was wearing.

The eighty year old mother of four, grandmother to four, and great-grandmother to four, didn't have a single hair on her head. As the old saying goes, she was as bald as a cue ball.

It was an unnatural condition, of course, which was brought on by monthly chemotherapy treatments for cancer. What was not unnatural was Lorene's acceptance of the disease that had befallen her, and her determination to make the best of it.

She expressed her forbearance in the simplest of words, "I have great trust in my Lord," she said.

"I know I have to die of something," she added. "But I don't have to give in to it. I don't have to give up. At least not until I have to."

Because she believed that with all her might, she did not give up, and she did not take to her couch, except, of course, on those few days a month immediately following chemotherapy treatments. Then she was physically knocked out from the effects of the drug, and nauseated almost to death. Then she had to lie down.

"I know that's part of it, and I get over it," she said. "I get over it because I know that it will go away. And when I get over it I start right back again, doing all the things I always do."

Those things included working two days a week as a lunchtime volunteer at a center for older Americans. She also delivered a daily hot lunch to a shut-in lady more than ten years older than she, and she stayed and visited with her.

"On Sundays I go to church in the morning and in the evening. I even bought a little white felt hat to wear, and everyone likes it so well," she smiled.

Mondays found her in the Buddha store, near her home, where she helped the owner, her daughter, June Waldon. The store had been in the Sallee family for more than ninety years. Lorene and her late husband, Clifford (Teedelo), operated it for twenty-five of those years. Every Monday Lorene shared the work there with Cheryl Spicer, a neighbor.

On Fridays Lorene joined a granddaughter for lunch and then they went shopping. Friday nights were usually taken up with card parties. She had recently attended a carnival at Bedford's Lincoln School; and she was looking forward to a hay ride scheduled for the next Friday.

"If someone comes along at the times when I'm not busy and wants me to go someplace, I go," she said. "If no one comes around, I bake. I'm busy all the time."

June and her husband, Bill, lived in the house next door to Lorene's, and Lorene took nightly supper with them. Were it not for their presence, their company, the things they did for her, life might have been more difficult. It certainly would have been lonelier, she knew that, and she thanked God for them.

"I thank Him every day, too, for being able to do the things I like, and for keeping me as well as I am," she further counted her blessings. "If cancer is what I am to die from, then that is my fate, that is what it will have to be."

Despite her spunk and all of her activities, and in spite of the kind efforts of her daughter and son-in-law, loneliness sometimes did creep into her life, she admitted.

"If I feel it coming I don't give it a chance," she said. "I climb in the car and drive to the store (only minutes from her house) and I talk with my daughter, or the people who come in there.

"My husband and I left there fifteen years ago, and there are a lot of people I don't know anymore. But I talk to them anyway," she said. "It helps."

Her husband died five years earlier of cancer. He suffered for months, was bedridden for months, and Lorene cared for him until his death.

She expressed concern that if I should write a story about her it should be an encouragement to those who might read it who are similarly afflicted with cancer.

"I hope that what you write about me will help someone else," she said. "I'd like for them to be able to take courage from it, and not sit and grieve. My doctor said I should do all the things I want to do. I'm doing them, and having fun. I'd like for others who have cancer to do the same, because it is a big help. If you give up you're gone."

CHAMPION RAT KILLERS

They were known as the "Champeens" who on a single Sunday afternoon killed as many rats as they could shake a stick at, until the carmine blood of the dead rodents joined that of previously slaughtered cows and hogs to run . . . Ah, but let's start at the beginning.

If you've never struck out on foot along graveled Old Slaughterhouse Road to skinny dip in the waters of Leatherwood Creek, or to walk its banks to a swimming hole known as Nine-Foot; and if you've never poked along Old Slaughterhouse Road to its end and into Old Cement Plant Road, just for the fun of it, or to hoot and holler at lovers parked in autos there until they fled, vexed and thwarted, the stage on which the great rat kill was enacted may be somewhat obscured.

However to begin at the beginning, a man named Ott Sieg owned the old slaughterhouse which stood just over the brow of a hill beyond 20th Street, high enough above Leatherwood Creek to provide efficient drainage into the creek of animal blood let there, and dripping entrails. Sieg rented livestock pens there to Bedford butcher shop owners who purchased beef and pork on the hoof from surrounding farms.

On given days of the week Sieg's slaughterhouse man, one amiable Charlie Brown, visited the shops in a horse-drawn wagon to obtain butchering schedules. Shop owners informed him of their needs — a slaughtered hog here, a slaughtered beef there— and Brown's work for the week was cut out for him.

Armed with a lasso and a machinist's ballpeen hammer, Brown snubbed and dropped the animals as efficiently and as easily as he hummed a tune that buzzed constantly and monotonously from between his lips. "Hmmmmmmm— ," and POP! the ball end of the hammer found its mark. No cow, no hog ever was frightened in its last few moments of life. Brown's ponderous benignity lulled them, however deceptively, into unguarded, trusting inaction, and suddenly they lay dead at his feet. "Hmmmmmmmm— ," POP!

Brown would then dress out the carcasses, and the spilled blood and drippings ran into the slaughterhouse drains and ultimately into the Leatherwood Creek. Bones were heaped upon heaps of bones outside the building, where rats, some as big as cats, daily and nightly feasted.

It was a pleasant diversion for Dutchtowners more than a half century ago— and many other Bedford residents — to hike out 20th St. and down to the old slaughterhouse to watch burly Charlie Brown go "Hmmmmmmmm—," POP! one older Dutchtowner remembered.

"One shot with that ballpeen was all he needed. And," he said, "those rats in that pile of bones— boy! Now they were really something. They piled up, and the blood and everything ran into the creek. And we used to go skinny-dipping there and it never bothered us. We never got sick. Never got a stomach ache. Nothing. And there was none of this ecology stuff then, either," he said.

Family names in Dutchtown in those days included, among others, those of Bahr, Isom, Endris, Abel, Krenke, Faulk, Rhoda, and Schuster. The limestone Grace Methodist Church now on the corner of 18th and H streets, in keeping with the predominant nationality of Dutchtown at that time, was in those early days called "The German Church."

It was to the daring offspring of many of the German families there that Brown one day offered a challenge. It had become imperative that the number of rats dining at the slaughterhouse be reduced forthwith.

"Come," he challenged the youth of old Dutchtown. "Come see how many rats you can kill."

And thus it was that on a bright Sunday afternoon the young men of old Dutchtown, armed with hammers, baseball bats and cudgels of all shapes and sizes, set off to enact what was to become a distorted and bloody version of the great event that occurred in Hamelin after Robert Browning dispatched his beneficent Pied Piper to that unfortunate city.

The young men of Dutchtown swung their clubs in and about the heaps of rotting animal bones until there grew in their midst a pile of dead rats as high as the renowned "Beanstalk" — believe it or not. So high was that pile of rats that, the next day, Bedford shook on its plattings as the old rattly-bangy flatbed press in its newspaper office printed under a bold black caption an account of the infamous slaughter.

"Champion Rat Killers of Dutchtown", the young men were called in the story.

It would be interesting to know their whereabouts today. They could tell the rat story in greater detail and they indeed could provide some information on the old cement plant, whose brick and concrete buildings then rose only a short walk from the old slaughterhouse.

Cement used in the construction of the Panama Canal was produced there, as well as cement for who knows how many other construction jobs.

Lex Reardon, who owned and farmed most of the ground around it in later years would have had some information, surely. And perhaps some of those workers who helped salvage the abandoned metal in and around the old brick and concrete buildings for World War II may have known something of the old plant.

Ariel Poling, and her husband Allen, and their son, Bill, who resided on Hidden Acres Drive, the extension of Old Cement Plant Road, were the owners of the land on which most of the remaining old foundations could be found at this time. The brick main office building of the plant had been converted into a handsome dwelling, and was at this time owned and occupied by Carl and Susan Beekman.

Ariel pointed out the poured concrete building in which dynamite was stored, the thick, heavy pilings on which conveyors once moved, a concrete tunnel which was used for some forgotten purpose, and the pyramid-like gray concrete pilings that stood like monstrous tombstones to this mystery of another time.

Ariel's father, Bill Megnin once owned the site of the old plant and a couple dozen acres around it. In one of the brick buildings he kept his horses in stalls he constructed therein. Their names still hung in there — Mack, Nell, Topper. And the name of another horse, Soapy, a strawberry roan once known to more Bedford residents than any other horse, was seen in many parades carrying his proud master Bob Conley.

Ariel was a gracious guide of the old grounds,explaining that the name of the site, which was "Opalacres" was in memory of her mother who, with Ariel's dad, bought the place about 1942 from Dr. Robert Smallwood. We walked under tall, whitening sycamore trees, thickening black walnut and wild cherry trees, and around scores of redbud trees. Some trees had grown between the concrete pilings so that their thick trunks choked the space in between the gray slabs.

If you've never walked that roadway or that creek-bank, you may want to do so some day. You will see many changes. And if you're in the mood to skinny-dip in Leatherwood there — have no fear; the old slaughterhouse with its animal blood and dripping entrails, and its pile of dead rats killed by those hailed "champeens" of long ago are no longer there.

WHEN JESSIE RAN THE STORE

Jessie Minnick said that she had done no great sight of traveling in her life, "But," she hurried to add, "I've been in several states." None, however, had a Freedom in it. A Freedom such as the one that throbbed with the extraordinary memories of the one in Owen County, Indiana. No matter the states to which travels may have taken her, Jessie always returned there.

"Anyone who ever lived here comes back, or at least wants to come back," she said in the cozy living room of her home in Freedom. "You miss these people when you're not here, and I'm always happier when I get to see some of them."

One would have to agree, they are somewhat special. Take for an example the freezing January night when a sleeping trucker's tractor trailer rig demolished the front of Minnick's Grocery Store on State Road 67 in Freedom.

"He just tore off the whole front of the place," Jessie said. "And, oh, it was cold. People came out and they put corrugated metal and tarpaulins over the big opening and closed in the store against that bitter cold.

"We'd had a Bell Telephone meeting in the store that night. We were trying to get phones in town. Later, after we went to bed upstairs, that truck, came along and wiped off the front porch, the front windows and wrecked the meat box. It was a nightmare of a thing. It was a Friday the 13th," she said.

Jessie, her husband, Herbert, and their four children, paid five hundred dollars in the early 1940s for the more than 100 year old building that housed the old ground floor store and second floor living quarters. They began operating a restaurant there, occasionally adding a shelf of groceries until that service outgrew the restaurant.

Horace and Beth Kay also operated a store in Freedom, a larger one than Minnick's. "It was a general store, where they sold everything," Jessie remembered. And she said of the Kays, "They were fine people. Good, hard working people." Horace, as did Jessie's husband, Herbert, conducted a huckster route in the surrounding countryside.

"We bought chickens and eggs, and we had feed and stock salt," Jessie said. "We had coal oil in a barrel that you pumped, and we carried just about anything anyone could need in groceries."

Jessie said the relationships developed between the Minnicks and the other customers became, "A friendly family sort of thing."

Chairs in which customers could sit and visit with the owners and other customers were always a part of the store's furnishings.

"People gathered in there," Jessie said. "They visited. They took the time to visit. There was a closeness between all of us. A community spirit."

Her thoughts suddenly shifted to the old Freedom School, leveled after consolidation with Owen Valley at Spencer.

"It was the center of our social life," she said. "We had our own basketball team. It was a small one, but it was a good one. And we could get enthused about it.

"Everybody knew one another," she continued. "In the large schools today you go to a commencement and nobody knows anybody. Back then you'd know every graduate. Of course," she noted, "there were only maybe seven to eleven of them."

Her mood deepened. "We lost a lot when we lost our school. More than just a building. And I can't see where we've improved ourselves by consolidating."

School vacation had ended one September when a nighttime fire destroyed the store and the upstairs living quarters. The frame, clapboard covered structure burned unhindered. Worthington volunteers who made the eight-mile run to Freedom that night doused nearby buildings to keep them from also going up in flames.

Jessie was to learn more about neighborly love after the fire.

"I had to hire some help to rebuild the store," she said of the concrete block structure then owned and operated by A. Z. West and his wife, Lenore, and where Dody Moore and Donna Thompson were employed. "But mostly," Jessie said with emphasis, "I didn't."

She said: "People just helped. One man did the wiring. Two men put the furnace in. They worked of a night, after their daytime jobs. And on the weekends. They rebuilt the store. They didn't charge me anything. They were just that way around here."

Jessie was thoughtful for a moment. Then she said, "There's a lot more good people in the world than there is bad ones. You just couldn't go on if there wasn't." Another slight pause, and Jessie said, "I hope I have no enemies."

An old friend, Marie Boyer, who operated the Shell Service Station in the center of Freedom said Jessie had no enemies.

"She saw some rough times back in those days," said Marie. "But she's been a real woman. And everybody just loves her."

At A. Z. West's store Dody Moore echoed the words of other community residents. "Jessie," she said, "is a sweet, lovely lady."

The community of Freedom has changed both in

appearance and ways since those days when Jessie ran the store. There are fewer commercial buildings in the town, and many of Jessie's old friends have been replaced by people she wouldn't know. Those who remain, however, are worth the staying in Freedom, they and the peacefulness.

Her son Charles and his family lived there, too. Mrs. Hobart (Margaret) Knoy, her daughter, was also there. She was the postmaster. And for at least part of the traveling Jessie did, another daughter, Mrs. James (Rita) Zaharako, lived in Florida.

"They grew up in the store," Jessie said. "And when we get together those days make good recollection."

She said she quit the store because, "I ran out of what it took to run it."

Approaching her mid-seventies, Jessie had witnessed many changes, and she missed those people who were gone. When she got to see those who remained — like at services at Freedom Baptist Church, or at the post office when the weather was nice enough for walking — she knew a profound satisfaction and happiness.

"But it's not like it was," Jessie said. "We got to see a lot of people in the store. At least we thought it was a lot of people."

BOWLING GREEN

A longstanding but questionable narrative about the former jail at Bowling Green described the holiday lynching inside the jail walls of a visitor whose crime, as proved in a mock trial, was the theft of an imaginary black cat.

June Clevenger told me the story one day while I visited with her and her husband, Waldo, in the antique-furnished oldest brick home in Bowling Green that was the Clevenger home in that small, unincorporated Clay County, Indiana community.

As the story goes, a quartet of petty criminals were being held in the jail one Fourth of July when the visitor arrived there. Because he had come to visit the four inmates as a friend, the jailer placed them all together in the jail's bullpen. Then, whether it was because it was a holiday, or because he had official business elsewhere, the jailer departed, leaving the group locked up and to its pleasures.

The mock trial is supposed to have ensued. The visitor, charged with stealing an imaginary black cat, was placed in the dock. Each of the four inmates presented evidence so damning against him, he was found guilty. And the court reportedly announced sentence, "to be hanged by the neck until dead," and administered justice then and there.

Bowling Green's jail, or at least the two-story brick that housed it at that time, still stands. The building was owned by the Clevengers, and at the time of my first visit there it housed each summer a collection of antiques offered by them for sale.

"Someone once asked me, 'How can you conduct a business from that old jail knowing that a man was hanged in there?'" June Clevenger smiled at the completion of her narration of the story. "I just told her, I said, 'Why should it bother me? I didn't hang him.'"

The bulky brick building, heated by wood stoves during its lifetime as a jail, was kept closed under lock and key during the cold months because it was too difficult to heat.

"I don't know how they managed to keep it warm," June said. "And I've always wondered about the sanitary conditions in there when it was a jail."

It appeared that the structure was built around and over a floor of slabs of sandstone a foot thick that made up its first floor. That floor, and the one above it were, in season, filled with the various antiques the Clevengers would put up for sale.

"I began my antique interest by digging for bottles," June said. "Bottles were a big thing. People went around to all the old dumps looking for them and starting collections. I was one of them. I went to all the old dumps here.

"There used to be a brewery here once, the Bowling Green Brewery, down on Eel River, and I dug around

The Old Jail Building At Bowling Green

143

that place for a long time, too, trying to find one of their bottles. But," she shrugged, "I learned later that in those days they didn't use them, that they used only barrels and kegs.

"Bowling Green was the popular halfway point between Bloomington and Terre Haute," she related more of the community's history. "Travelers could make it by wagon or on horseback from Bloomington or Terre Haute to here in one day. And they'd lay over here," she said.

To care for the needs of travelers, seven hotels and seven taverns had been established to serve them. The seven taverns were supplied by the brewery on Eel River. One traveler who remained overnight during the Civil War in one of the hotels known as the Chaney Building, and who probably partook of the Eel River brew, still enjoyed a dubious fame. Robert Gay was arrested and tried at Indianapolis for spying on the Union. He was convicted and shot. Bowling Green history notes that Gay's was the only known such death in the west during that war.

Two years after the Civil War, the town sported — in addition to the jail, brewery, hotels and saloons — two churches and one under construction, two Sabbath schools, one literary society, a business college, a printing office, a Masonic lodge, three temperance organizations, and the usual early collection of stores, smiths and shops. A courthouse stood in the center of its small square.

Because of its proximity to Eel River, Bowling Green had come to life as a trading post in 1812. When the Clay County seat was moved from there to Brazil in 1877, the change marked the beginning of the end for the incorporated town. With a total population of about two-hundred souls at the time of my first visit — according to Lowell Sheese, the town's post master for the previous thirty years — and an increment of tumble-down structures, there was little remaining indication of its golden season.

One of the falling-down buildings was a rambling, gaping victim of vandals. It once was the Washington Township School. June Clevenger, who was born in Bowling Green, graduated from there in 1942. Three years later the school was vacated as the result of consolidation, and Bowling Green saw an end to its identity in high school athletics.

Despite the decay, the town has not been unkind toward those who sought livelihood and contentment there. Former garage and filling station owner Millard Huber was one of these. When Huber celebrated a century of living, a greeting from President Carter found him a bed patient in his home. But Huber still took three squares a day, read two newspapers, and viewed television as avidly as its best fans. He and his wife, Elizabeth, shared a neat little home that was situated on what was left of the public square.

The Clevengers were also among those to whom the small community on State Road 46 west of Spencer had been good. After more than a year of the store, Waldo and June shut the place down between Christmas and the New Year. "We were able to give ourselves a Christmas present, a week's vacation," June said.

They were spending it in the comfort of the brick house that was built in 1845, in rooms that were more than eighteen by eighteen feet square and furnished with handsome antiques.

"Our friends think we're kind of weird," June said. "They can't imagine what I'd want with all this 'stinking and musty old furniture.' Well, they don't all fit together," she gestured toward some of the old pieces, "but we like them. And we love to come home. That's why we took the week's vacation.

"I've been going through drawers and looking at stuff I haven't seen for a long, long time," she smiled with satisfaction. "And if we live long enough, we've got trunks of stuff — oh, so many things, like quilts — I'm going to do someday, and things."

Among their plans was the restoration of the jail.

"It'll still be an antique shop," June said of the business that already had attracted dealers and buyers from several states including Texas. "But we want to fix it up."

A part of its restored charm undoubtedly might have to include, however dubious, the retelling of the hanging of the jail visitor inside the old building's walls. Whatever the inclusions, June looked forward to the restoration project with a cautionary reminder once quoted by an acquaintance who then was in her eighties.

"I know," she had told June, "that there are not twenty-four hours in a day anymore."

During a more recent visit with June, she told me of an elderly woman who kept several "cat houses" in Bowling Green, one of them in the jail while the old woman lived there.

"She loved cats and she had lots of them," June recounted. "When the place got unbearable to live in any longer she'd move, and after she would leave a building she would have it torn down."

It was from the cat lover that June purchased the old jail for twelve hundred dollars.

"It was a mess," she remembered with a wry face. "That old woman kept her cats in the cell block and I cleaned it up all by myself. That was a job and it took a long time."

In the years since my first visit with her, June had

kept so busy weaving rugs for sale, and buying and selling antiques that the old jail, even though it was still standing, had yet to be restored. Waldo was gone from Bowling Green and left to herself June was sharing a home with her daughter, Charlene Hauser, who had assumed her mother's hope of one day restoring the old jail to live in. "There is space enough on the first floor of the two story brick building for three rooms in addition to a large family room in the area occupied by the cell block. The upstairs floor is one large room that can possibly be made into several rooms," June said of the building's potential.

Because it gave up its city status after the Clay County seat was moved to Brazil, Bowling Green has had little or no growth. The community's post master at this time, a friendly cooperative lady named Brigit Browning, estimated there were some sixty homes in the community sheltering a population of approximately two hundred souls. Four hundred boxes inside the post office along with a single motor route eighty miles long serve the office's mail patrons. Browning counted the businesses there: "A Bronco Shop, one beauty shop, one co-op, one restaurant, and one donut shop," she said.

June told an aging, rather unclear and misty story of bank robbers who long before the turn of the century had cached a chest of stolen money on the banks of Eel River at the edge of Bowling Green. The location was known at one time because a woman was said to have sat on the site daily, protecting it until the robbers should return to claim it. According to a spiritualist in more recent times, the woman was still there.

"I spoke to her," he is alleged to have said. And when asked if she were still there, he replied, "I guess she's still there. She's been there since 1877."

Another rumored but enduring tale is that of an

alleged itinerant card-cheat who, at the height of Bowling Green's hey-day, was shot and killed while playing cards in one of the seven taverns. Before his body was interred at Six-Mile Cemetery, it was placed on public display, and school children reportedly were paraded past it and admonished to note, "What sin can do for you."

"There are lots of stories," said ninety year old James E. Campbell, who at the time of this most recent visit lived in a beautiful wooded retreat outside of Bowling Green on State Road 46. "When the school burned in the early 1900s, I went to class in the jail. The first through sixth grades went there until they could get another school built."

Campbell left Bowling Green at age twenty-one and returned with his late wife, Adeline, after he retired. On his return he began keeping scrap books on Bowling Green. At this time he had twenty-three, three-ring binders of information he had collected.

"FUEL MAN"

Had you asked directions to his home, a Popcorn neighbor more than likely would have said, "You mean 'Junior' Arthur?"

That is how they knew him, had known him all his life. But to the rural mail carriers — and for this introduction — he was Everett. Everett Arthur.

"This is the center of Popcorn," he told my wife, Marion, and me in affectionate tones and with a sweeping gesture of one arm. And having grown up there, almost everyone knew him, or knew of him.

As a boy he skinny-dipped and fished for suckers and catfish in Popcorn Creek. When he was older and stouter he carried two one hundred twenty-two pound cans of milk, one in each hand.

He did that many a day when he hauled milk for Harry Armstrong from surrounding dairy farms to Johnson Creamery and Spriggs Dairy in Bloomington. And he made a host of friends. Same thing for jobs he held with Pal Deckard at Fifth and Lincoln in Bedford, and Wayne Hammond at 14th and K streets there, and Eva Crulo in Avoca.

Add twenty-seven more years to those, years during which he delivered fuel oil for Mullis Petroleum Products in Bedford on a route that extended from Jackson County to Odon, and the years total a bunch. And all those jobs, all those years, combined to bring him a veritable fortune in friends.

"I had a hundred and twenty-five stops on the fuel oil route," he said. "They called me 'Fuel Man.'" And beginning in 1964 the appellation carried over to his CB radio communications. "Breaker! Breaker! Fuel Man!" A CB alert that was very popular.

In his retirement at his Popcorn home, the CB continued to receive a large portion of his daily attentions.

"Hey Fuel Man," someone would key up with a call to him. "Did you get your potatoes dug up today?" And the conversations went on and on.

"I like my CB," Junior said of how much he enjoyed visiting with friends by radio, and how quickly the CB would help an otherwise long day in the country to pass.

He digressed briefly to recall events on the oil route when the CB was a valuable assistant, how it challenged the monotony of miles of driving, and how now it had become an enduring companion in the extended hours of retirement.

"When I'm using my CB, midnight will come pretty quick," he said with satisfaction.

During the early days at Popcorn, his mother and father, Chloe and Everett Arthur Sr., were among the many who helped build the Oak Grove Pentecostal Church. Chloe had ensconced Junior on a pew there while he was still a child. And still an adherent to that early Pentecostal teaching when we visited, he said, "It is the only way to heaven for me."

Along the way he met a pretty young lady named Delight Hayes, and she became his girl. It was so she could hear more clearly the stirring foot-tapping and hand-clapping music there one night that he had propped open the church door with a rock.

So carried away by the joyful sound and rhythm of it was she that she became a member of the church, joining him in frequent spiritual celebration there.

After having been together forty-three years, they continued to attend services there. Having played a guitar ever since he was a boy, to its accompaniment and that of church pianist Delores Baker's playing, he and Delight continued singing together at that same church.

"We have a good time at church," he said. "We go

early so that we can practice." And inadvertently providing a clue to what church probably ought to be, he added, "It's a lot of fun. We have such a good time practicing that sometimes we can't tell when the fun stops and church begins."

The Arthurs, who lived in the Monroe County section of Popcorn, had a daughter, Cathy, who with her husband, Greg Baker, and their family, lived in the Lawrence County area of Popcorn. It so happened that where they all lived, near the joining of Popcorn Road and Snow Road, the two houses were just a short walk apart. The proximity of each house to the other made for a pleasant family arrangement; frequent visitation for the adults and grandchildren.

Despite the nearness of one house to the other, unfortunately, a telephone call from Monroe County to Lawrence County was a long distance toll call. Fortunately, however, they could and did use their CB radios to communicate.

During our visit he asked if we would care to hear him play the guitar. And just that quickly three voices in harmony to "I'll Fly Away," a typical Pentecostal song, filled the room; Arthur's, Delight's and Marion's. (I don't sing.)

For our further pleasure he took us all back many years to the days when he was wooing Delight. "I serenaded her with this song," he said, and he played and sang "Little Indian Nappanie."

None of us could be sure of the spelling of Nappanie, but some of the words were:

"My pretty little Nappanie,
"Won't you take a chance and marry me."

Though they lacked the sparkle and enthusiasm of youth, the words as he sang them were still full of love and — a quality that youth learns only over many years — devotion.

Retirement can be such a wonderful time and the room seemed to sway with the good feeling of it. The music brought unspoken dear memories and a sense of forever. And for the space of a few moments the hospitable Arthur living room in that part of Popcorn in rural Monroe County, Indiana, had become another world.

Please look in the back of this book for a list of all of Larry Incollingo's books and how you may obtain a personalized gift or autographed copy of one or more of them.

AUGUST KNOPF

August Knopf was only fifteen years old when he went into the stacking yards at Oolitic as a water boy.

A few years earlier, on his first day at the old one-room Oolitic School, he had told a teacher, "Ich kan nich lessen, ich kan nich shieben, ich kan nich sprack-en."

Boys from laboring class families from countries around the world were expressing in their native tongues to teachers in Oolitic, Bloomington, Bedford and surrounding communities those same words: I cannot read, I cannot write, I cannot speak (your language).

They came from their native lands to work in stone; the homogeneous mass of Indiana limestone that underlies that entire area, perhaps even the house in which you are now reading this.

They came by the dozen, by the score, and by the hundreds, for in those days much manpower was needed to remove the blue, gray, buff and variegated stone from its natural bed.

It took men to man the many mills — Hoosier, Joyner, Rowe, Kerber, MacMillen, Dickerson, Salem and Walters, and maybe a dozen or so more — where that stone was sawed and cut and fabricated for buildings around the nation. Name a famous building, and don't be too surprised to learn that Indiana Limestone was used in its construction — Empire State Building; Tribune Tower; Chicago Mart; State House in Jefferson, Missouri; Radio City; Victoria Hotel in New York City, New York; Post Office in St. Louis, Missouri; and scores more.

Accompanying his mother from Germany aboard a Cunard liner when he was eleven, August Knopf could not see the part he would play in the construction of this new country. But at this time, at seventy-five years old, and carrying a severe wound of that dangerous trade, he was able to look back on his role in building America, and to know a degree of satisfaction and pride.

In the history of the world, in that of America and little Oolitic, August Knopf, until my visit with him, was one of the dozens, the scores, the hundreds of nameless who shared that satisfaction.

He logged in his mind a record of some of his contemporaries in those hardened fields — Nat Joyner, Merle and Robert McClellan, Spencer Norton, Rudolf Link, Ben Pointer, Jim Pointer, Stacey Stultz, Henry Delpha, Marion Hicks, Ab Lee, Andy Pope, Lincoln and Harry Beyers, Roscoe Enlo, Ell Blackburn and Marshal Owens, superintendents, foremen, hookers, sawyers, power men — men from all phases of that old and aging trade, legions of men whose names are too numerous to recall here.

John L. Walsh was another of those early men. It was Walsh who indirectly brought August Knopf to Oolitic. Walsh had offered August Augustus Mack, a Wisconsin stone carver, the job of fabricating the stone for the Milwaukee Railroad Station in Bedford, and Mack took it, taking to Oolitic with him his wife, Anna Rosalie Knopf, August's sister.

Siba Carmichael, too, must be included, although he operated a saw mill, but the wood he sawed was used in the booming stone industry. Siba appeared before a bondsman and affixed his signature to a document which stated that should August Knopf run away, commit a crime, or be anything but a well-behaved alien in the U. S., Siba must forfeit three thousand dollars cash.

August was well-behaved all his days in the U.S., including those long, long days that became three months on Ellis Island while immigration authorities unraveled red tape. And when the Nazis invaded Poland, August, on the advice of his wife, Zilla Mae Owens Knopf, became a citizen. Zilla Mae, whose life and livelihood turned on stone, is buried in Hopkins Cemetery, north of Oolitic, a small, well-kept burial ground surrounded by now idled quarries, and not too distant stone mills.

In the idiom of their survivors, many of those who are interred there are "buried in the quarries" which, interpreted by a newcomer, could mean they have gone back to that which gave them life, or at least that which gave them sustenance in life.

From water-boying in the stacking yards, August, seeking to better himself, won an opportunity to work in a mill, sawing huge quarry blocks into slabs.

"Sawyers," they were called in the trade; those often wet, sand-grimed men, who guided large quarry blocks onto platforms and, swinging a six-pound hammer, set the gang saws above them. Gang sawyers, the men whose sweetest music was the rhythmic zung-zung of the rocking gangs.

"We had no diamonds (saws) in those first days," August remembered back through the years. "You had to know how to feed sand down into the cut to cut the stone. We'd average twenty inches in twelve hours."

When the diamond gangs were introduced the sawing was faster, "And if we didn't get one down every six or eight hours our bosses wanted to know why," he recalled.

At forty-nine years of age, far from the boy he was in the stacking yards, and head sawyer at Kerber Mill — a mill of gang saws only — "I got busted up," August began recounting his only serious mishap in his years in the stone industry. A swinging gang struck a two-by-four, driving it into his right thigh, crushing it.

Doctors held little hope for his life but wanted to amputate his right leg, but Zilla Mae, who was alive then, said, "No. If he's not going to make it I want to bury him with two legs."

August had seen men killed — crushed — on the gangs. He was to live to see more.

His injury left him with a definite limp, but he continued working far past normal retirement age. Then one day, August went to his superior and said, "I just can't make it anymore." And he left the stone industry. He sold his home in Oolitic and moved to a stone block house at 2917 "V" Street, in Bedford, which was owned by a nephew.

He and Zilla Mae had no children, and retirement days may have got lonely, sometimes, and the nights long, but August Knopf, as do all men, especially those who have labored physically hard all their lives, said, "I'm happy to be alive at seventy-five."

He obviously meant it, for his blue eyes lit up behind his glasses, and he ran a hand carelessly through a thick shock of grey hair, and he smiled. And at that very moment I remembered 'way back, sometime in the early part of my visit with him, that he said, "You set eight gangs with a six-pound hammer all day and you know you've been someplace."

August Knopf, as had that long line of men and boys who came from foreign lands to Indiana to work in limestone, to help build America, had indeed been "SOMEPLACE."

A Banquet of Short Stories
MOORE'S VARIETY

You could feel the weight of disappointment in the words as the retired Whitey Tackett spoke them: "No candy kisses?" he said looking from Ike Young to Bob Moore to me.

"They're on order, but they haven't come in yet," Bob said consolingly.

"They've got peanut butter in them; they're awfully good," Whitey had spoken directly to me before forlornly turning and walking out of Moore's Variety Store in Gosport.

"I've got two tons of candy ordered," Bob spoke through the disappointment that still hung heavy in the store. "But Whitey, he likes candy kisses."

Whitey could have settled for something else. An old fashioned candy case in the store was literally filled with delicious candies: chocolate haystacks, malted milk balls, burnt peanuts, Boston baked beans, chocolate coated peanuts, hot cinnamon balls, bridge mix, peppermint lozenges, red hots (Imperials), lemon drops, candy corn, tasty sticks, orange slices, lollipops and other sweetmeats.

Even the glass front of the candy showcase looked good enough to eat, and five year old Chad Smith ran his tongue over its surface while he tried to stretch his little arms around the whole collection. Moore's candies were a tempting sight, including the former penny candies which now sold for two pennies.

Chad got a whole bagful before he left the store with his mother, Mrs. Willie (Connie) Smith, of Stinesville. Chad's little cousin, Tabitha, daughter of William and Mary Smith, Ellettsville, who was with Chad and his mother, also got a bagful of ten pieces of two-penny candy!

Memories of filled candy cases and bagfuls of penny candies swirled and reveled in my head until I was

157

sure I was going to ask Bob to fill up a bag for me. As Chad and Tabitha were pointing to the candies they wanted and the tiny treats were being dropped one by one into the small brown paper bags, I was aware of a total understanding of Whitey's disappointment. When with filled bags in hand the children skipped happily out of the store, I found myself wishing that for Whitey's sake there could have been some peanut butter filled candy kisses in Moore's that morning.

In the days of penny candies, bolsters were a favorite of mine. They were like a small Clark bar. I could put a whole one in my mouth, its ends poking my jaws out so that I looked like I had tried to swallow a broom handle crossways. When I could no longer restrain myself I'd let my teeth sink into the sweetmeat, releasing in my mouth a mixture of chocolate coating and crisp peanut butter and molasses and corn starch filling. My mouth salivated like a rogue sugar tree then, and in order to get enough capacity to hold the sweet flood there I'd have to seal my lips and pooch them out past the end of my nose and try to chew. Bolsters were such a taste delight.

My other favorite was a peanut butter filled caramel called Mary Jane. I can never forget that candy. When I was expecting my first son to be born I was shocked to learn that something had gone wrong and my first son was not my first son but a tiny girl with long black hair.

No one expected a girl. No one had thought of a name for a girl. When the decision fell to me I could think only of the other favorite penny candy of my childhood — Mary Jane. So, without another thought I exclaimed, "Let's call her Mary Jane."

The reverie was brief. I heard Ike saying that, "The October wind was blustering like a March day," outside. He asked if I was acquainted with a popular

uncle of his who lived in Bloomington. Ike was helping Bob in the store on this morning and, for a seventy-five year old retiree, he was pretty active help. He
once had a grocery store adjacent to Moore's in
Gosport. When he retired eight years earlier Bob
knocked a hole in the wall that separated the two
stores and made Ike's place a part of the variety store.

Ike's name was Lee, and I asked if his middle name
might be Isaac, if that's where the nickname Ike came
from. "No," Ike said. "There was a time when everyone in Gosport had to have a nickname, and they
called me Ike. I have a brother whose name is Estel,"
he continued. "His nickname is Brigham."

Moore's was an interesting store and I used to like to
visit the place when my job took me to Gosport. No
junk, everything in its place so that a visitor could look
straight ahead, up, down, sideways, and see something
bright and new and colorful, something useful. There
was so much stock there a fellow would have been
hard put to begin listing it, but I do remember bright
yard goods, brown ware and blue willow ware.

I held my breath there one day as I watched Bob
carry a heavy boxed set of the blue willow ware to a
counter. A few minutes before that he'd unbuttoned
his shirt to show me a protrusion on the right side of
his chest under which there was a pacemaker.

A year before that visit to Moore's, at sixty-four, Bob
had that thing implanted after he got sick. If he had
heart trouble he didn't know it, for it wasn't that kind
of sickness. But his doctors believed that's what the
root of his problem was. Since its installation he'd
had no more trouble.

"I don't even know it's there," he said of the pacemaker. "I get a checkup every six months, and after
three years I'll get it replaced."

After caring for Bea Marley who came in to have

159

some prints made from a color negative, we talked some about the new signs that had been put up around Gosport. There were new white on green street signs, black on white speed limit signs, white on red stop signs. One had caught my eye, a street sign that read West Lousisa Street. I thought it should have been Louisa, but more than one sign read Lousisa, and I wondered if it were named after Lousisa Somebody. Then Bob said he'd like to retire, and start drawing "some of that social security."

Which brings me to the sad part of this story. Moore's Variety Store was for sale. The Moores had been in that store since 1922 — Sam Moore, Bob's father, and his brother, Allen. Bob had taken over in 1945.

"I'm tied down, and I'm at the age now where I don't want to be. But, I'd probably be lost away from here," Bob said.

Ike, who was standing nearby listening, pshawed that. He said: "I wasn't lost when I retired. I missed the people for a while. But now I can lay down and go to sleep anytime."

That sounded like a vote of confidence for retirement. And when Ike said, "I don't even feel like seventy-five," I figured Bob was in pretty good company to see him through the sale of the store and into retirement. Before those two events would occur, I thought to myself, it would be nice if Bob would get some peanut butter filled candy kisses for Whitey.

Moore's eventually was sold. Unfortunately, as such things go, the sale proved its death knell. In my future visits to Gosport, I was keenly aware of its loss. Even now, these many years later, when I am in Gosport I remember Moore's Variety Store, and Bob, and Ike, and Whitey, and the old fashioned candy case and little Chad Smith running his tongue over the glass front of it.

TAYLOR LETTELLEIR

He appeared as tireless as the great industry to which he'd given a lifetime, and as rugged. As he moved through the skidway, cutting anchor holes in squares of Indiana limestone, the dust of dozens of majestic structures respectfully cushioned the soles of his ankle top shoes. And from a lofty seat in a moving traveler above the skidway, operator Dan Smith gave wide berth to his proud head.

Taylor Lettelleir was sixteen when he took the job in a long-ago stone mill that would bring him, more than fifty-three years later, to the Matthews Brothers Company mill near Ellettsville.

The parade of mills that passed under his tireless feet in those years included Bowman & King, Shawnee, Alexander & King, American-Oolitic, Hoosier, South Side, and a host of others now fading in the history of Indiana limestone's glorious past.

The buildings he helped create — that stand and will stand for an eternity — include the Tribune Tower in Chicago, the State Office Building in Richmond, Virginia, the U. S. Archives Building and the Washington Cathedral in the nation's capitol, and many others across the continent.

At lunchtime, over a sandwich of thin-sliced bread and lunch meat, he looked back over all that time, unimpressed. He and his wife Irene had seven children, and cutting stone was a job, a good job. Some of the best stone cutters the industry had ever employed, will ever employ, were old men when he became an apprentice, he said. And, he added, in the years that followed, he worked with some awfully good stone cutters.

"They were cutters who used mallets. Men who refused to use air, the pneumatic hammers we use today," he paid them a special tribute.

Lunch Break For Taylor Lettelleir

"When you have a large family, it takes a lot of work to raise them," he said. "And at one time back then, we were the highest paid craft in Indiana. We made a dollar and twenty-five cents an hour, while carpenters were making fifty cents and plumbers sixty cents.

"Then," he continued, "World War II came along and there was very little stone work, and we fell behind and everybody else got ahead."

Stone cutters at the time I visited with him in the stone mill received five dollars and seventy-two and one-half cents an hour. Planermen got two cents more than that, gang sawyers got four dollars and sixty-five cents, traveler operators four dollars and eighty-two cents, and machinists five dollars and forty-nine cents.

"It's been worse," he said with a shake of his head. "There were times when we went through those Depression days — boy, when you went through them you went through something — if you had a job there were ten thousand other people after it."

Lettelleir was seventy-two, a waymark in life he had reached one month earlier. After seven years of semi-retirement, when in order to obtain a Social Security pension he was restricted in his earnings, he at this time was free to earn as much as he pleased.

"It doesn't bother me," he said of the eight-hour days. "Except that my feet get a little tireder than they used to.

"But I believe if a man is healthy, if he feels good, he ought to work past sixty-five."

He pulled in his chin slightly to accent his words.

"Now I don't say he ought to kill himself. But he ought to work, and he ought to work at what he knows best."

Lettelleir was following his own advice. What he was doing was what he knew best. It was where he fit best, where history would find him, among the Harold Hardens, the Don Hoards, the Garold Arthurs, the Vernal Mobleys, the Ray Grays, the Delbert Stogsdills, the Don Medleys, and the long line of dusty men of the Indiana Limestone industry.

There where the sounds of life were the zung-zunging gang saws, the humming travelers, the buzzing pneumatic hammers.

There, where immortality was measured by the height of a building in a far-off city, and the depth of the stone dust under his feet.

A MILLION DREAMS UNFULFILLED

To the left and right of the lectern, banks of flowers reached almost to the ceiling of the rural church.

More than four hundred mourners, an entire community, sat silent, pensive, solemn, shocked.

Their mood deepened as six boys dressed in black walked slowly, solemnly down the center aisle of the church, bearing between them a white casket. Reaching the lectern they carefully turned to the left.

The throbbing silence was broken by a giant shush of breath and a muffled sob. A second white casket and six more bearers, comparably dressed and equally sedate, moved slowly, carefully down the aisle.

Standing, hands gripping the lectern, the minister watched through misty eyes as they turned to the right.

A spray of red roses, the life and death symbol of love, was placed on each of the caskets, and again the awful silence was broken as the youthful bearers, eyes downcast, now walked almost hurriedly to their seats.

The minister raised a white handkerchief to his eyes. He cleared his throat.

"In the house of my Father there are many mansions. . ." he began softly.

In the lonely darkness of the closed white caskets the bodies of a girl and a boy lay cold, unhearing, dead.

From somewhere near the country church a rooster crowed. The throaty, raucous sound stealing a moment of the crestfallen air.

Only hours before, a piercing, blood-chilling sound had ripped through the quiet night of the community. When the sickening scream of skidding tires, the grating crash of metal on metal, the discordant treble of shattering glass finally ended, a dreadful sepulchral silence followed. And then it was learned that two lives had suddenly been stolen.

164

A boy and a girl.

Not children, but yet not old enough to have known the pride of casting a vote for a President of the United States.

Old, and yet too young to have known the sweetness of love and life, of toil and gain, of loss and hope.

A million dreams unfulfilled.

In the pulsating red lights of ambulances and police cruisers, a midnight highway was suddenly turned into a loathsome kaleidoscope of carnage. In flashes of light and darkness, shattered glass, twisted hulks of metal, scattered headlights, fenders, doors, dead and broken bodies, ashen-faced policemen, formed a wretched, illusive pattern.

Violent death.

In the darkness of night.

High above, smoke from burning flares, caught in the lights of halted traffic, hovered over the scene like a shroud. The acrid fumes, the cries of the injured, the last of a glorious life flowing rich and red down a hillside, the gathering curious. All these found their place in the ugly, piteous panorama of nighttime tragedy.

From somewhere among the spectators a fearful, quavering voice: "Oh, my God! My son was out in a car tonight. I wonder if that's him."

Ambulances moved and the injured were on their way to a hospital. Only the dead remained.

Only the dead.

And the living who could not leave the dead. The dead who were so young and so alone, and so . . . so . . . dead.

And the living, whose duty it was to identify and, reluctantly, notify.

The living, who would knock softly, and haltingly deliver the message that would bring unspeakable grief, the message that would live in the memory of loved ones for as long as memory remained.

The living: shocked, incredulous.

An empty bed which in the space of a single, choking breath became a cold monument to pain and despair.

Two white caskets side by side.

"Oh God!" A voice overwhelmed with sorrow cried out. "It's like a serpent coiled around my heart!"

A floral bank of sorrow and loss.

The warming glow of youth and beauty turned gray and cold.

"In the house of my father there are many mansions . . ."

VALLONIA

When cookies came in bulk my favorite was the wine cookie. Why they were called that is still a mystery to me. They were big and round and you could help yourself to two, out of a large box, for a nickel.

Another nickel got you a slice of round longhorn cheese and you'd have a wine cookie and cheese sandwich.

The circumference of the cheese was greater than that of the cookies and it stuck out all around. You had to nibble that away before you could get to the sweet stuff.

Still another nickel bought a soda to wash it down. Then you had the feeling that you'd feasted like an admiral; the best food that money could buy. At least the best that three nickels could buy.

It used to be a treat just to think about those sandwiches and secretly salivate until you could save up three Indian head coins. Not anymore. Most cookies come in packages now. Rows and rows of shelves upon shelves of them in the supermarket — all well beyond the reach of three nickels. And you never see wine cookies.

As a matter of fact, you don't see Indian head coins anymore, either.

These thoughts came to mind as we stood in the Vallonia Gas and Grocery on State Road 135. Since we had stopped there two years earlier, Jennifer Everage, owner with her husband, Sam, installed a short deli case. The food looked so tempting, neatly trayed and covered. Jennifer had prepared everything the night before.

"Except the chicken salad," she said. "I fixed that this morning 'cause I had to cook the chicken first."

We succumbed. The portions were large. While we were stuffing, a man came in and studied the deli offerings. Finally he said, "Cut me a slice of that round cheese and give me a slice of bread."

That was all it took; visions of wine cookies and cheese charged out of a dusty corner of my memory. It excited me so much to remember all I've written above that without introduction or a by-your-leave, I began relating it to the stranger. But before I could finish he slipped out the door with his slice of cheese and bread, and was gone, probably because he had only a very short lunch break.

I thought to narrate the same account to a lady who came in after he left. But in just a few seconds I became aware that she had fresh hog manure on her boots, and to preserve the taste of my chicken salad sandwich, baked beans and banana pudding, I moved into another part of the store. By the time we finished eating we agreed Jennifer was a great cook.

Curiosity had taken us to Vallonia; Fort Vallonia Days would begin the next Friday: the 25th anniversary. It was a quiet day and we used our time there to renew old acquaintances. Jennifer was first. Then Carol Wheeler, at Wheeler's Bait Shop. Wheeler's had sold the lucky lottery ticket to Keith Pawling who won nineteen thousand dollars one Saturday night on the Indiana Lottery television show. They were awarded a one per cent bonus for having sold the ticket, Carol said.

She told us that recent rains had just about washed Fort Vallonia away. A small stream you can normally wade or jump across had become a raging torrent. The thing ran under Myrtle Blackwood's tiny restaurant, under the road and through the old fort.

When we walked over to see her, Myrtle warned us to be careful. There was a large hole we could have fallen through in the floor behind the door, and another larger hole at the back of the room. In the glare of a bright light set up down there we could see the muddy stream gurgling over its rock bed under the building.

About a foot or more of the flooded stream had covered the floor during the rain and Myrtle showed us the high water mark on the white refrigerator. She opened the door to show us how much sand had washed into the appliance. Then she recounted for us how she saved a man from the high water down there.

She kept hearing what she thought was a call for help, she said. The sheriff lived across the street from the restaurant and Myrtle alerted him. "I hear somebody hollering like they're desperate for help," she told Sheriff Herschel Baughman.

Somebody was. A man had gone into the creek, then under the store and under the road, to clear debris from the subterranean stream and had become trapped under the road as the stream suddenly swelled. Responding to a 911 call, four or five fire trucks and some fifty volunteers arrived. The quickest way to reach the poor guy was to cut a hole in the restaurant floor, which they did. And the sheriff and a deputy crawled down and brought him out.

"If I hadn't heard him hollering, he would have drowned down there," Myrtle said. "He was snagged on something. His whole body was underwater except for one side of his face; he had it turned so he could breathe." After expressing his gratitude, the rescued man observed, "It was scary down there."

Myrtle, who has been "thirty-nine, and a little more," for many, many years, suffered from crippling arthritis. Refusing to yield to the affliction, she forced herself out of bed every morning and went to the little restaurant. Although she didn't cook anymore, she did sell a few candy bars and cigarettes, and enjoyed talking with visitors.

"I won't give up." she declared. And in parting she advised, "Don't go to bed except to sleep. Then get up the next day and go on."

SNOWDEN GIRDLEY

It would have required several people to join hands to reach around the trunk of the mammoth soft maple tree that rose from Sarah Plummer's shaded front yard in Burns City.

Snowden Girdley stood on his front porch some distance away, his attention directed to the tree by a visitor.

"Oh Lord," Snowden sighed a quiet, throaty exclamation, "I don't know how big around you'd say it is. I know it was there, big, almost big like that, I guess, when I was a kid."

Girdley was crossing the threshold of eighty. Before entering his own home he took another look at the giant maple, "I just don't know," he mused.

The dimensions of the natural colossus were perhaps better left to the imagination, so I wrote off the unanswered query to follow Girdley into the old aluminum-covered frame house that was his home. But it was worth one more look, an over-the-shoulder pop-eyed kind of look, and a few clucks, which I dutifully gave the big soft maple.

It was a moment for grandiose sights, for when I entered Girdley's living room, I was confronted by a lusty philodendron that reached from pedestal table to ceiling.

"Wow!" I exploded, leaning backward to better see the rising heart-shaped leaves. "How?"

Girdley pointed to what he called "a wooden doily" under the vessel holding the roots of the giant plant. At one point, on the edge of the wooden doily, someone had drilled a hole into which had been placed the butt end of a long narrow sassafras pole. And it was that pole, and the stub ends left from smaller branches cut off it, that supported the tall green growth high above our heads.

"It was my wife's idea," he recalled the woman to

whom he was married for thirty-seven years before her death. "She said one day, 'You're good with tools. Why don't you figure a way to keep that plant growing up.' And that's what I came up with."

Given the time and the space, it occurred to me, Girdley's philodendron might one day have achieved the dimensions of Sarah Plummer's soft maple tree. Maybe even those of the beanstalk in the story of Jack and the Beanstalk.

But the leafy thing was not why Girdley had led me to his house in his 1969 model pickup truck from Mike Pridemore's grocery store. And he tore my stare and speculations from the growth by calling my attention to a mountain of hand-crafted, hand-rubbed, black walnut lumber resting on tulip poplar rockers.

"Here," Girdley was saying as he pulled protective covers off the huge chair, "Sit down. Just try this, and see what you think of it."

I backed into the cavernous space between the wide-spaced, inviting arms. My bottom side rested easily on the twill-woven hickory bark that made up the seat. My arms rested on the high chair arms. I suddenly felt very small inside the monstrous thing, and then just as suddenly I saw myself a sovereign, a ruler of a vast universe, seated high and mightily over Girdley and the tiny world about him.

It was a great boost for a hard-working reporter, and I liked the feeling.

"How much?" I asked Girdley.

"Three hundred dollars," he said without a stammer.

I slipped out of that monstrous throne into Girdley's tiny world again.

Newspaper reporters just don't make that kind of money.

"It's beau-beau-beautiful," I told him. "But it's nah-nah-not for me."

Girdley nodded. "I know," he said. "I made it for somebody else. He already has one I made him for two hundred dollars."

The chair took hours and months to make, and Girdley did it all himself in the workshop housed in an outbuilding at the side of his home. He took me out there to show me around, and he waved a hand at the assortment of power and hand tools he had.

"I just go on buying tools like I'm always going to be here," he smiled. Then he added, "I'm well pleased with myself. Here I am, seventy nine, and I go on working in this workshop making all sorts of things."

I took a second look at Girdley for the first time then. Trim, chesty as a bantam rooster, with light and dark shades of thick gray hair standing almost straight up, rolled-up shorts and rolled-down socks, he hardly appeared to me, then a younger man, the octogenarian he was about to become. I took another look at the shop. It was clean and, much to my own chagrin, neatly kept, with a place for every tool and every tool in its place.

He must have sensed my envy, for he said, "If you're going to hobby around in wood like I do, you need to know how to care for tools."

There was another outbuilding on Girdley's lot, an old falling-down smokehouse. We climbed onto its rickety porch-like platform and through the sun-dried, ancient door frame. The ceiling inside seemed to hang precipitously close to my head; the walls gave evidence of having once been papered.

"A man and his wife used to rent this from us when Maxon Construction Company was building the Crane ammunition depot," Girdley said. "It was Burns City Ammunition Depot back then, and this town was twice its size with the people that came here to work.

"You could rent out anything that had a roof over it,

and everybody did. We got ten dollars a week for this. A man could make seventy-five cents an hour back then, and that was a lot of money," he said.

Girdley was born a couple of miles from the small Martin County community, and his entire life had been spent either near the town or in it. He, too, worked for Maxon, and later at the Crane Naval Ammunition Depot, as did many of those who lived in the community on the eve of World War Two, and in later years.

JULIA PARKER

Picturing in my mind the richly woven fabric of her memories as she spoke them to me (. . . born in a log cabin near Hickory Grove . . . a life shadowed by toil and trial after the untimely death of her mother . . . loyal to the teachings of her heart . . .) I couldn't help but marvel at Julia Parker.

Beginning as a six year old surrogate mother to three younger siblings, she nevertheless made time for three loves: God, family, and the banjo. And as an eighty-four year old great-great grandmother, she not only was still true to them, but in recent years she had added another — oil painting.

Though the wonder of rearing her own family of six and the continued daily care of a paraplegic son at their home on R. 3, Springville would make an inspiring story of itself, there is the exhilarating account of the banjo. Heard by many in her years of appearances throughout south central Indiana, at her fingertips it made an uplifting, if not toe-tapping, unforgettable sound. And for thirteen of those years the moving strains of her banjo could be heard far and wide on Sunday afternoons over WSLM Radio, Salem.

Julia strummed it there with the Evening Light Gospel Singers, a family group made up of two of her daughters and their husbands, Brenda and Lowell Flynn, and Wilma and Warren Swango. The group at this writing was still intact. And Julia — affectionately known in the group as "Gran'maw" — still was strumming her eloquent banjo with them.

"When I was a child I had a friend show me the G, C and D chords on a guitar," she said of an early interest in music. "Then when I was nine years old I ordered a fiddle-neck guitar out of the Spiegel catalog for nine dollars."

174

Music became for her another means of praising God, and she played and sang hymns at various churches. At sixteen she married Evett Parker and they lived in a corn crib insulated with flattened cardboard boxes and empty twenty-four pound paper flour sacks. While her husband worked on a farm for one dollar and a pint of milk a day, she gave birth to their first child there.

Although she had never touched one, she had a deep yearning through the years to play the banjo. Finally, at age fifty, despite her husband's cautious advice that she might be too old to learn, she sent away to Montgomery Ward for a four-string tenor banjo. To her husband's surprise, she not only learned to play it, she forsook that instrument for a five-string banjo she later ordered out of a Sears catalog.

"I had someone show me the G chord on it," she remembered, "and after my husband would leave for work in the morning, I would pick up that banjo and practice playing it until daylight. Then I'd do those things I had to do around the house, but I couldn't wait to get back to that banjo."

When she felt accomplished enough, she joined the Evening Light Gospel Singers on radio. She remembered trying to remain unnoticed by staying in the background of the group. But it wasn't long until she was up front playing breaks. In addition to the years on WSLM, the group was making as many as four other appearances a week, and spending weekends playing and singing at area churches.

"I wasn't ready to quit," Julia said of a seemingly boundless energy befitting a person half her age, "but the long drives were tiring. We never charged anyone for playing, and," she laughed, "the cost of replacing broken strings was getting expensive."

175

Julia's talent for oil painting surfaced unexpectedly and her work attracted a wide following. Beginning early and ending late, her long days were exhausting. When I inquired of her source of energy, her heartfelt reply was true to a life-long conviction.

"If I didn't have God I couldn't keep up," she said. "He is my life. From the time I was a child I have never known anything but to trust in Him for all I want or need."

To obtain an autographed copy of one of Larry Incollingo's other books turn to the back of this book. Have a copy personalized for a loved one or a friend.

JOHN STEWART

There was a time in Nashville when John Stewart built houses for five hundred dollars each. There was no electricity in them, no lights, and their exterior walls were only weather board tacked to sheathing. But they were adequate shelters in which people could live and finish to their liking as the means to do so became available.

Then zoning and planning came to Nashville. John shook his head. "They started telling a feller what he could build and what he couldn't build on his own property," he said. "And that is when I said, 'The hell with it. I'll just set on the Liar's Bench at the courthouse.'"

John's memory of Nashville went back apiece, as he put it.

"This place was a mudhole in the spring. And in the summertime it was so dusty you couldn't see a car on the gravel roads," he said.

He also remembered a day when his carpenter father inadvertently exposed a one hundred dollar bill while making a purchase in one of the town's shops.

"No one," John said he remembered the merchant exploding to his father, "ought to make that much money."

Thanks to the action of the zoning and planning commissions, John became one of Nashville's more colorful characters. On a nice day visitors could see him smoking a cigar while seated on the Liar's Bench. But more than likely he would be seated on the bench in front of the Hob Nob Corner Restaurant at the corner of Main and Van Buren streets. He might even have been seen leaning back on the bench on the Brown County Federal Savings and Loan Association patio with his feet propped upon the surrounding wall.

John Stewart

At seventy-nine, tall, angular, and attired in khakis, plaid shirt, insulated vest, and western style Stetson hat, John was a pleasant sight in downtown Nashville. Sharp featured and with an aquiline nose that hooked slightly over a ready smile, he even was a charming attraction. If he was not familiar with all of the town's natives, he at least was acquainted with them, and he always had a word or a dozen or more words for them when they passed.

For the ladies who passed, John kept in a vest pocket a sack of nuts from the Jack and Jill Nut Shop over on Van Buren Street. And for the pretty ones who dared to dip into it, avowed Billy Salmon, then executive director of Brown County Recreation and Industrial Development Council, Inc., John provided each with a supporting one-arm hug.

"Billy," smiled John, "is a mighty fine feller."

Then in a subdued voice, John appended that statement with the lament that, "About all my buddies is gone. Jack Woods, Lloyd Voland, and ol' George Coakley. And Ethel, my wife. She died in 1963 after we were married for forty years.

"No children," he shook his head. "But we raised plenty. Somebody else's. Gave them a home. When we was doing that, and helping other people, driving them to the doctor's, I wondered who'd ever take care of me if I ever needed it. Well, now I've got several young friends who do a lot for me. When I get sick they come see about me.

"This, "John indicated Nashville with a sweeping gesture of one hand, "is the greatest place on earth."

Then, as an afterthought, he hurried to add, "In the country."

Had a visitor to his bench showed enough interest, John carried in the other pocket of his vest a packet of black and white, and some colored, photos. They included snapshots of himself in the company of Jack Woods, Bill Woods, Dan Marshal, Mary Staehr, Sen. Richard Lugar's mother, Bertha Colwell, and photos of his wife, Ethel, with her dog Tippy, George Bixler's daughter, Kelli, on her pony, John's father with a team of mules, and a yellowing photo of a niece the name of whom escaped him.

There were two warring factions of businessmen and politicians in Nashville at this time, and friend-ships were being tested. One group that considered itself progressive was interested, among other things, in improvement and modernization. The other felt that Nashville should retain the quiet, the peace, the beauty of old, and yes, the trees.

Many words were exchanged. Some of them almost threatening.

There was a common ground. A place of tranquili-ty, acceptance and friendship. The Liar's Bench.

The same Liar's Bench that John Stewart sought out when he said, "The hell with it."

But only a John Stewart could have seen the wis-dom in such a step.

CLARICE JACKSON

There are probably few people around now who remember that a demure lady named Clarice Jackson used to play the piano at the old picture show in Owensburg.

There are probably fewer who remember there once was a picture show there.

Movies were innocent in those days, no nudity, no four letter words, and maybe more exciting and fun than the filth portrayed on the screen today. They were silent films in those days and the sound of music made them better and was welcome.

"There were two or three guys with me who played violins and a guitar," Clarice told me one day. "We played anything, just so it was music, and we kept it going."

The movie house was in a former canning factory which was situated across State Road 58, below the old Monon Railroad depot, later the Cleve and Mary Smith residence.

Clarice once operated a restaurant in Owensburg, and more people may remember her for that. It had no name. One was not necessary. Anyone in and around the small Greene County community who had a yen to eat out knew the place was there, and that it was Clarice's. Kids from the old Owensburg school provided a substantial portion of her business.

The closing of the school brought unwanted changes to Owensburg. The greatest of these was probably the loss of vibrancy that young life, with its host of pleasures and problems, brings to a community.

"Until then there'd always been a school here," Clarice said. "When I went to school it was on a hill behind the Baptist Church. It had four rooms. Some of my classmates were Roy Roberts, Lewis Roberts,

Clarice Jackson

Luella Fordyce, Audrey Wade, Jessie Smith and Merle Hudson. There were three teachers, George Reagan, who was also the principal, Clovis Henderson and Lester Laughlin."

Clarice's husband, Alfred, barbered in Owensburg for more than forty years and, according to Clarice, "He cut just about everybody's hair."

Her father, Luther Hall, was co-owner of an earlier Owensburg store and Clarice recalled the first time she'd seen chewing gum.

"It came in packages of five small cakes — like Ex-Lax — and the brand name was 'Too-Loo,'" she said. "It was kept in a glass jar on a shelf in my father's store. Every time I saw it there my mouth would water for the sweet taste of it. But, a girl who chewed gum in those days, or wore silk hose, was considered a 'flapper,' and not very nice, so I didn't have any. But how I wanted some," she sighed at the still aching memory.

When in subsequent years her father learned of her childhood craving and her painful self-denial, he smiled and said, "If you wanted some so badly why didn't you ask? I'd have given you some."

Luther built a new home at Sexton Springs, adjacent to the land on which Lilburn Owens, for whom Owensburg was named, had earlier raised a log cabin.

"Mr. Owens lived there in the log cabin with his wife, a jolly old lady everybody called 'Aunt Pop,' and she smoked a pipe and chewed tobacco," Clarice remembered. "Mr. Owens was an old man and he could hardly see or hear.

"One day I left my big doll lying in the yard and he came by and saw it," she began a recollection of the man. "He picked it up and brought it to the house. He told my mother, 'Mrs. Hall, I found this child a-layin' out in the yard. I think it's dead. I do believe it's dead.' We laughed over that."

Clarice also laughed when she recounted her reaction to having seen her first automobile.

"Something went up the road just a-flyin'," she remembered, "and I called my mother. 'Mom!' I hollered. 'A buggy just went up the road and it didn't have no horse attached to it.' My mother laughed and told me that it was an automobile."

JACK OF ALL TRADES

In a small cemetery adjacent to a Pentecostal Church in the Chapel Hill neighborhood, a number of tombstones carved to resemble tree trunks bear no mark of the master who created them.

Those who've seen tree trunk-shaped headstones may now know that those, at least, were the handiwork of one W. Dallas ("Bud") Sowders who was born and raised at Chapel Hill, and whose body now lies at the foot of a much larger but less artistic tombstone in the same cemetery.

Around his flower-covered grave, when I visited there, stood a miniature picket-like fence which was painted white, and carved on the stone to the left of his name was the name of Cora, his wife, who had died in 1948.

Bud Sowders died at the age of fifty-five in 1928, ending what his daughter, Mrs. Mary Brown, of Bloomington, described as a life in which "We felt like we knew him forever."

Bud was a twin: "He was named William Dallas and his twin sister was named Susan Alice," Mrs. Brown said. Susan Alice married Chesley Chambers.

Although Bud's occupations were primarily those of farmer and quarry blacksmith, he was a jack of all trades, and could do almost anything, his daughter said.

"I remember," Mrs. Brown recalled one of his happier accomplishments, "he took an old steering wheel from a car and set it on top of a pole in ball bearings and tied long ropes to it so we kids could have a swing. It was a May-pole, and we'd never seen one and we always thought Dad invented it," she said.

When folks who lived in the country around Chapel Hill needed help they came to Bud. If they were in need of a casket in which to bury their dead, he nailed one together out of native wood, lined it with bleached muslin and gave it to them as a gift. The tree-trunk tombstones were, for the most part, also gifts to those who could not afford to buy them.

"He wasn't a stone carver by trade, but he was able to carve them," Mrs. Brown said.

True, he may not have been a carver in the strictest stone industry interpretation of that job classification, but he nevertheless carved handsome tombstones.

During World War I, Bud operated a steam-driven grist mill on his farm. When folks took their wheat there to be ground, and the ration stamps which gave him federal permission to grind it, he always ground some extra for them, saying, "It's their wheat, why shouldn't they have enough flour." And he never charged them for grinding the extra amount.

"On Saturday it was like a parade coming to our farm," Mrs. Brown recalled. "People came from all over the country to have their wheat ground. Dad would start before daybreak and keep working until after dark. Mrs. Alva (Pearl) Rush used to come there. She'll remember those days."

Mrs. Brown said Pearl walked miles from her home to Bud's mill, carrying a sack of wheat on one hip and her child on the other.

Dr. George Mitchell used to travel by horse and buggy from his home in Smithville to Chapel Hill to tend to the sick. Lake Monroe wasn't even a dream back then and the trip was considered short, over a dirt road that cut across what is now Fairfax Beach.

Mrs. Brown as a girl attended the Valley School in that same vicinity, crossing and re-crossing a covered bridge to get there and back home. Clarence Stewart was her teacher in the old one room school house.

"The Hawkinses, Sowders, Kinsers and ragweed

just about took over Chapel Hill in those days," Hansford Stewart recalled with a laugh.

They must have been good days, for Hansford added, "The dirt there was so poor you had to have a pint of whiskey to raise a fuss on it."

George Cracraft had a chestnut orchard there then, too, and used to ship chestnuts all over the world.

Bud once put legs on an old oil drum, cut a door into its belly, cut a hole in its top and stuck stove pipe into it and used it for a stove.

"Dr. Mitchell always said he invented the barrel stove," Mrs. Brown said. "It wasn't long after my dad made that stove until everybody in the country had one."

Bud made an iron man, too, to help him cut wood with a cross-cut saw.

"He had a spring on that thing and every time he pulled that saw that iron man would pull it back again," his daughter laughed.

Bud's mother was alleged to have been part Indian and possessed the power to cure thrush in infants. This was supposed to have been passed on to her son but he never used it.

He was a man who could make anything, and if he was in need of a particular tool and didn't have one, he made it. Such was the case with the tools he used to carve flowers in the stone fireplace of the old Cleve Hillenburg house, a large brick on Old State Road 37 south of Bloomington.

"I was only fifteen when he died," Mrs. Brown remembered, "but he was so active and did so many things for people and for us it seemed like I knew him forever."

A VIEW FROM THE STAGE DOOR DELI

The thought left my mind as unruffled as the flag that hung down in faded, twisted stripes under the brass ball on the pole outside the Owen County Jail; as unmoved as Spencer had been that morning.

From a window table in the Stage Door Delicatessen, breathing in the tasty aromas from the hot grill, I wasn't worried. Winter, I tried telling myself, was still miles and miles away.

"You'd better go home," from a far corner of my mind I could hear the warnings again. "This looks bad."

In time I did go home, and before I got there I'd wished I'd done so sooner. Before I heeded the warnings, sudden freezing snows had whipped Spencer with a stinging fury, leaving its streets, its walks, its trees and utility poles a mass of ice, and me stranded there, alone.

No aloneness equals that of being alone wherever you might be in a winter storm.

"You'd better go home," I again heard those worried voices from that corner in my head.

I wondered if this particular winter would be as severe as the previous winter. Where would the snow and ice catch me next?

I wasn't really worried about it until it was almost too late. Surely winter was not miles and miles away, as I had tried to tell myself. It had arrived.

It was cold outside now. I took my notebook from my coat pocket and opened it on the table in front of me. From my seat I was able to see a man step out of the jail door, wrangling his arms into the sleeves of a coat as he walked. He took a tin out of his pocket, tilted it, and filled his lower lip from its contents. Then he was gone from sight. I touched the hot drink on the table in front of me.

I was reminded of the heat I'd felt earlier. It had embraced me like a warm blanket in Bayh's Hardware, a warm blanket touched with the pungent smell of burning coal. The longer I remained in the store the more comfortable I felt.

Outside again it was colder. And I had shivered. Money's Store had been warm, too. And Chambers Restaurant. The Towne and Country Shoppe. The Ward catalogue order store. The Owen County Courthouse. The public library. Emerson Furniture Store.

All felt and smelled of artificial heat, the harbinger, the promise of winter. I walked to the Stage Door Deli, where I took the window table, from which I could see the jail, the limp flag, and at which I had begun writing.

I saw Pat Brinson having difficulty with a parking meter. He hit it with the heel of his hand, dug into his pocket, put another coin into it, struck it again with the heel of his hand. It seemed that his actions were automatic; he dug and hit, dug and hit. Later, standing almost in the middle of South Main Street with him, I had asked Pat why.

"I put fourteen pennies in that durn thing and got only a little better than an hour out of it," he said leaning heavily on the walker he used to get around. A dime, two nickels, would have gotten him two full hours. "I don't know what's wrong with it," he frowned.

Pat had suffered from arthritis. The last six years he'd gotten around on crutches, canes, and, finally, the walker. He'd had operations on his hips, and steel balls were installed in his hip joints. They were supposed to make life better for him, help him walk. I asked Pat what he thought about those surgeries, those steel balls.

187

"These makeshift things don't work as well as they tell you they will," he said sorrowfully. "They're not like what's supposed to be in there."

Pat was waiting for a telephone call, or a letter, that would tell him they were ready to operate on him again — to try to fix him up well enough to walk as well as any other sixty-two year old. Until they did, Pat expected to be on that walker, an aid which he said was safer than crutches or canes.

Ray Lockwood was involved with a meter on South Main Street, too. Only he wasn't trying to buy time from this one, he was leaning on it, resting while talking with Jim Clark.

Ray and I met after he'd accidentally lost a leg in a farm tractor mishap. The words I remember best from that first meeting were those that made up his promise to walk into my office as soon as he got his artificial limb. When that day came he waited out in his truck while Lillie, his wife, came into the office and asked me to step outside.

Ray had his artificial limb, all right, but there were some adjustments to make before he could walk well enough. He apologized for disappointing me. That touched me deeply. There with Jim, Ray had an arm draped over the parking meter, and one of those metal crutches gripped in his other hand.

Jim was eighty-six years old the past October, and he got around like a man at least twenty years younger, maybe better than that. He also drove an "El Cameenee" from his home on Texas Pike to Spencer, and always, always, Penny, his pet fox terrier, shared the ride with him.

Jim's wife, Marietta Alverson, had taught school in Spencer, Montgomery Township, Bedford, and Clinton before she was stricken with breast cancer. Jim himself had been county clerk, councilman, township trustee, school board member, cattle farmer, and auctioneer.

As a young man he'd gone off with the American Expeditionary Forces in World War I, and served in France and Belgium. Jim had a few dramatic observations on being eighty-six.

(1) "There was a time when I knew pert near everybody in this county. Now I don't know my next door neighbor."

(He also knew the reason for that. It happens to those who dare to live long enough to outlive their contemporaries.)

(2) "Ain't it awful when a man's mind will slip like mine?"

(3) Smiling: "They can say what they want. When you're eighty-six life ain't much fun anymore."

Marietta died in 1971 after surgery and suffering for ten years. Jim devoted himself faithfully to her care during that time. He also took care of several relatives who became ill and later died. Those folks in and around Spencer who were old enough to remember had a lot of esteem for Jim. They thought he was quite a man.

T. Perry Wesley told me about it one time, but this blustery, snowy day was the day I saw the art display in Emerson Furniture Store on the south side of the square. It was a collection of award-winning paintings from 1952 through 1976, all done by Owen County artists. Bob Emerson, who gave me my tour, explained their presence there.

To generate traffic in the store and to further promote interest in art among the county's talented, Bob's mother, Helen Emerson Wesley, conceived the Owen County Art Contest, he said. There was a doubting Thomas — Bill, Bob's older brother who wagered his mother five dollars the contest would not attract twenty-five paintings to the store. The first year drew at least thirty-five, and subsequent yearly contests varied between thirty to fifty paintings. As the years went by, more and more establishments exhibited paintings, and the Owen County Art Contest was discontinued. But what a run it had! Twenty-four years.

Winners included, among others, works by Doris Bond, Charlotte Allbritton, Iva Ekey, Olif Pegg, John Higer and Alma Edwards.

Mrs. Wesley's interest in art went far beyond that first contest. "I remember when I was a small boy," Bob gave an indication of that period, "she'd have her easel set up in the living room and have about ten artists in there painting and talking about painting..."

I not only was able to make my way through snow-covered, frozen Spencer later that day, I was also able to make it safely home where I put these notes I made from the Stage Door Deli window together for my next day's newspaper column.

TRUE LOVE

Fay Hicks held up her left hand. The third finger was adorned with rings. One, she said, was given to her by her husband, Stanley, before they were married. The others were also gifts from him, including a wedding band to replace the worn original. Last Christmas she received still another from Stanley, a diamond nestled in a bed of rubies.

"It's a dandy," she exclaimed as she held it up in the living room of the Hicks home north of Needmore. She added candidly, "I didn't need it. But," she smiled, "I appreciate it." She slipped it onto another finger.

Generous, thoughtful husbands who give their wives gifts are not rare. But how many of them continue the practice, say, after having been married a lifetime? Stanley and Fay had been together for nearly sixty-six years.

"I just wanted to get her something nice for Christmas," Stanley said of the newest ring. "I like to buy her things."

It goes without saying, really, that in order for a marriage to last so many years two people have to live a long time. Stanley was eighty-eight, and Fay was ninety-two. What needs to be said, and repeated, though, is that when two people who are wed so long look back, their years together, as Stanley and Fay noted, invariably add up to one brief interlude.

Something else. Stanley expressed it in this manner: "I never thought I'd live to be in my eighties."

Does anyone? But it happens. Quietly, unobtrusively, the years can and often do pile up. Suddenly there they are, a whole long lifetime of them. Yet, said Stanley and Fay, time need not pilfer all the glories and joys along the way; one or two, perhaps, but true love, as it did for them, will prevail.

191

"The best thing that ever happened to me was marrying her," Stanley still insisted. "And looking back over the years with her I can't think of a thing I would change. One more thing. When you live for the Lord you have contentment in your life."

Fay agreed with all of that, except that if she could have made a single change it would have been in her age. "I'd like to be sweet sixteen again," she said whimsically.

Stanley's life began simply in East Oolitic. He was a quarryman, auto mechanic, and, for twenty-three years until his retirement in 1964, he worked at Central Foundry, in Bedford.

A twin in a family of eight girls and two boys, Fay was born in Eldorado, Ill., graduated from Jonesboro College, and taught in a one room school at Earl, Arkansas, until she moved to Lawrence County. She was sewing men's shirts at Reliance Manufacturing in Bedford when she met Stanley. She later was also employed at Central Foundry until a baby-sitting problem sent her into retirement.

"Stanley was working on the day shift and I was working on the night shift," she explained. "When I went to work I took our baby to the plant gate, where I'd meet him. I'd give her to him, and he'd bring her back home and care for her until I got off work."

They had three children, two daughters and a son. One of the daughters lost her life in a freakish off-road one-car auto accident. Her death was the single painful chapter of their life together. Her children were among nine of Stanley's and Fay's grandchildren. They also had eighteen great grandchildren.

There have been other losses. Fay's first love died of influenza during World War I. She had also lost seven siblings.

An older sister, Goldie Beard, who was one hundred

years old, lived in Arkansas. Fay's twin, May Freeman, a widow, lived in Ft. Wayne. She was married to Perry Freeman. Fay explained that he was a brother to Frank Freeman, whose widow, Marie, lived in Williams.

"I went out with both of them before May and Marie married them," Fay confided with a smile. "But that was before I met Stanley."

For ten days some time prior to my visit, including her birthday, Fay's life hung in the balance at Dunn Memorial Hospital.

"The doctor gave her about three hours to live when I got her there, unless he could put her on life support," Stanley said of that experience. "It's a kind of miracle, in a way, that she's still here."

Asked if she had any advice for those seeking lasting love and longevity Fay replied, "I'm not old enough to give advice. I don't want to get that old. But I would tell people to live."

Concerning her long marriage she added this: "We've had a wonderfully good life. And I'm just the same old me."

A HAND FROM THE GRAVE

At a young people's party in a country church one night, a youth sought to enliven things by daring any one of his companions to take an ice pick from out of the church kitchen and plunge it into a grave in the nearby churchyard cemetery.

The weird suggestion was met with hoots and laughter by the other young men and screams from the girls. But after some talk, one of the fellows agreed to do it, if a friend would go along with him.

"No! No!" Some of the young people shouted. "That wouldn't be fun. Someone should go out there alone."

As might be expected, the girls shrank from the thought. Though the young men did not shiver and shake and scream as the girls did, none volunteered to accept the dare.

"You go," one of the young men said to another.

"No, you go," his friend replied.

"Don't be silly," the girls screamed. "Not on your life," they shouted.

Finally a pretty girl stepped forward, her face flushed around an almost brave smile. She looked from one to another of those gathered around and she said, "I'll do it."

There were loud cheers and screams.

"Go! Go!" The guys shouted encouragement to her.

"No! No!" the frightened girls screamed at her.

The pretty girl whirled suddenly, her long skirt flaring slightly above her attractive ankles as she turned in the direction of the kitchen. When she returned she was carrying the ice pick.

"No! No!" screamed the girls.

"Yes! Go!" shouted the young men.

There was no turning back now. The pretty girl was committed. She opened the church door and stepped out into the dark night alone.

As the door closed behind her, a hush fell over the group inside the church. During the breathless silence the floors and the walls creaked and popped. A rose of Sharon bush outside brushed its leaves across the window in a swishing of goose-pimpling sound. From somewhere inside the building a cricket fiddled a nervous tune.

Suddenly the small sounds were gone, a long wailing scream taking their place. The young men and women were petrified with fear, their eyes fastened on the church door. But it did not re-open. They waited a long time— an awfully long time, but the pretty girl, the brave girl, did not reappear. At last one of the girls said they had better go out and check — find out why the pretty girl had not returned. But there was a great deal of hesitation before anyone moved, and then everyone moved together.

They went out into the dark night, slowly. They called out the name of the girl. They received no answer. They inched their way toward the churchyard cemetery, very slowly. Suddenly one of the girls screamed and raised her hands to her eyes. Then another and another of the girls screamed, until the night convulsed with piercing sound.

One of the young men, braver than the rest, ran forward. Then another young man ran forward, until finally everyone was gathered around the still form of the pretty girl where she lay dead atop a mounded grave.

Later, after the fright had been screamed and cried out of all the young people and they had telephoned for help, authorities found the ice pick. The fine shaft had pierced the hem of the girl's long skirt as she knelt to drive it into the grave, pinning the garment to the sod.

Although an autopsy was to disclose the cause of death as cardiac arrest, authorities said the pretty girl's death might be better attributed to fright. They speculated that failing to notice that she had accidentally pinned herself to the ground, she probably thought she was being restrained by an avenging hand that had reached up out of the grave.

LEFT-HANDED GHOST

One late night — at two o'clock in the morning to be exact — a sleepless Bloomington father and son were sitting in the kitchen of their home sharing a pot of coffee. Seated across from each other, they spoke in quiet tones, as people will do late at night like that, of unimportant things. Both men were right-handed, and each had his cup of coffee sitting on the table next to his right hand. At a now forgotten point in the conversation, the father reached for his cup with his right hand. It was not there. The cup was near his left hand.

The men's eyes met across the table. Without a word the son watched as the father removed the cup from in front of his left hand and replaced it on the table in front of his right hand.

In the ensuing silence, while the two men watched without a word passing between them, the cup mysteriously moved from in front of the father's right hand to a point in front of his left hand.

The house was situated in an old residential section of the city and had been occupied by the father and son shortly prior to that night.

Incredibly interested in what they had witnessed, the father and son immediately set out to learn as much as possible about the past occupants of the house. Their search was long, but their diligence eventually paid off. They found out that the widow of the original owner, who had outlived her spouse by more than a half century, was an insomniac. And they learned that it had been her habit to prepare and drink coffee each morning at two o'clock.

Their research also unveiled a curious fact. The elderly widow was preparing to enjoy a cup of coffee at two o'clock one morning when death quietly overtook her. The date was June 14.

Father and son checked a calendar. It was at two o'clock on the morning of their first June 14 in the old house that they had witnessed the moving coffee cup.

Could it have been that the old widow might have been seeking to enjoy one more cup of coffee before her final departure from this world?

The father and son believed so, for they continued to witness this phenomenon every June 14 since the first time they saw the moving coffee cup. And to cinch their belief, they said that their search of personal information about the old widow also revealed the fact that she was left-handed.

THE HEADLESS CALLER

A resident of Burgoon Ridge in Polk Township in Monroe County was awakened late one winter's night by sounds outside the snowbound house she shared with her husband and large family.

Lighted kerosene lamp in hand, she went to the door and opened it to the cold night and stood there looking outside. She saw the form of a man, arms outstretched in her direction, taking steps toward the house, but getting no nearer with each step. Yet she could hear each step he took, as his boots c-r-r-unched the snow underfoot. Closer examination of the strange form brought a gasp to her lips. The man was headless! However she looked at it, his body began or ended at his shoulders.

She hurriedly gathered the tail of her long flannel nightgown in her free hand, hooked a trembling, naked leg around the door, and kicked it shut behind her, leaning her clammy body against it in fright and disbelief.

The woman returned to her bed. But not to sleep. The next morning at breakfast, her husband and children sat enthralled while she narrated the nocturnal experience. As she spoke the final word of the eerie account, there was a startling knock at the door she had slammed in fright the previous night.

When the woman's husband opened it, a relative stood in the opening. He couldn't come any sooner because of the deep snow, he apologized, but he had a message for the woman. Her brother, he said, who lived a few miles away on Axsom Branch, had been the victim of a recent hunting accident.

He had rested his shotgun against a fence and as he began climbing over the strands of wire, the firearm accidentally discharged — blowing his head off.

199

FALLING TOMBSTONE

During a visit to Liberty Cemetery, a small hillside church burial ground in western Jackson County, I discovered this sober reminder on an aged tombstone:

"Remember friend as you pass by,

As you are now so once was I.

As I am now so must you be:

Prepare for death, and follow me."

Unknown to me at that moment was a strange drama that had unfolded only a few days before in which the same verse had played an eerie role. Here is what happened.

Three year old Jonathon Schafer and some little companions were playing in an old cemetery near their home in Noblesville.

No one could be sure how it happened, but a large tombstone toppled over and fell on Jonathon, pinning him, critically injured, to the ground.

Jonathon's friends, although shocked at the sight of their little playmate lying under the big tombstone, had the presence of mind to run for help. They attracted the attention of a neighbor who then was passing in her car. She quickly ran to Jonathon and lifted the tombstone off him. She also summoned the child's mother, Karen, and an ambulance.

"He was badly hurt," Mrs. Schafer recalled at St. Vincent Hospital in Indianapolis, where her son had been taken after the mishap.

She and her husband, James, an attorney, were given little or no hope for their son's life when they reached there. Jonathon was bleeding internally from a lacerated liver.

The child survived emergency surgery and was admitted to the hospital's intensive care unit. In days his condition improved.

His mother described his survival as a "miracle."

"There wasn't a whole lot of hope for Jonathon," she said. "But everyone in our neighborhood had been praying for him. His survival has reaffirmed my faith in God."

Looking back to the day of Jonathon's almost fatal accident, she recalled that "The tombstone falling on him that way gave me the creeps."

The tombstone marked the grave of one Ambrose Moody, a three year old boy who was born in 1894 and died in 1897. At first glance the date of his death appeared on the aging tombstone as October 7, the same date as Jonathon's accident. But the engraved letters that made up that date had faded and weathered and may have formed another month— possibly December.

Chiseled into the stone below that date, however, were the words of the verse I copied from the tombstone in Liberty Cemetery, miles from where Jonathon was hurt, but with some slight variations. It read:

> "As you are now,
> So once was I;
> As I am now,
> So you will be;
> So prepare for death
> And follow me."

After seeing that, Jonathon's mother remarked, "It was freaky."

There's more. When the boy's grandfather, William Schafer, then composing room general foreman of Fort Wayne Newspapers Inc. went to see the accident site, he tried to lift the fallen tombstone but couldn't, his daughter-in-law said.

The elder Schafer, a six-footer who weighed two

hundred and forty pounds, said, "I could lift only one end or the other."

He estimated the stone marker weighed at least two hundred pounds.

How, then, was the neighbor, a small woman, able to lift the stone to free Jonathon?

When she returned to the cemetery the day after the mishap, she tried to lift the stone again. She couldn't budge it.

"The cemetery is an old family burial ground in the middle of our neighborhood," Jonathon's mother explained how her son happened to be playing among the tombstones.

"We worry about our children being hit by cars, or that they will fall out of trees, or that they will fall into the lake (there was a lake nearby). Then something like this happens," she said. "It makes you wonder. It was a terrible thing to go through. Thank God for our neighbors; they are really wonderful people."

There's still more.

When Jonathon was being admitted to the hospital's intensive care ward, one of two nurses there introduced herself as Catherine Ambrose.

The Schafer's caught their breath. They immediately thought of the name on the tombstone that had fallen on their son: Ambrose Moody. However, although the nurse did pronounce her name Ambrose, she spelled it Ambrouse.

Could there have been something prophetic in Jonathon's strange experience. Do such coincidences stem only from the child having been in the wrong place at the wrong time? Was it simply one of those freaky, creepy, unexplainable things that just happens?

MORE UNCANNY TALES

There are no facts, and certainly no photos to support what you are about to read. I have no documentation of these events except that these were accounts sent to me, or told to me, by readers.

A despondent young woman in a cemetery near Burns City one night walked to the grave of her younger brother, who had met a tragic death, and whom she missed very much. Once there she proceeded to slash her wrists and to cut her throat. Then, for some reason, with blood spurting from those wounds, she ran screaming from the grave, scaled a fence surrounding the burial ground and fell into an abandoned cistern on the other side where she succumbed.

Searchers scoured the area for days before her dead body was discovered. She was given a proper burial in a grave next to the brother whom she missed so much. Now on nights when the moon is full, nocturnal visitors to the cemetery have claimed, a voice from the direction of the abandoned cistern can be heard wailing repeatedly, "Let me ou-u-u-t !. Please let me ou-u-u-t!"

***

On certain nights of the year, the bridge on the road leading to the old slaughter house east of Bedford reportedly is the scene of the grim re-enactment of an early Lawrence County crime. The form of a huge man, carrying a lighted lantern in one hand and a human head in the other, crosses and re-crosses the bridge afoot.

***

A tragic accident in horse and buggy days was said to have happened in the covered bridge that spans

The East Fork of White River near Williams. A frightened horse is said to have reared, lost its balance, and crashed through the planking wall of the bridge to the rushing water below, taking the buggy and a small child with it. The animal and the child perished together.

In later years nocturnal sparkers near the bridge claimed they had been interrupted by a woman attired in a bonnet and long skirt who raced through the bridge screaming, "Mary! Mary! Mary!"

***

Near Spring Mill Park east of Mitchell, the limestone walk leading to an abandoned house was a topic of lovers' tales. Approaching the building arm-in-arm, lovers have been unable to keep their feet on the walk. It moved — swayed, heaved — and tumbled them to the ground. In each reported case, the moving walk prompted a speedy retreat from that trysting place.

***

A young man and his intended returning from a church service in eastern Lawrence County, were frozen into immobility one night as they were about to cross a bridge that spanned Leatherwood Creek. A shapeless white form floated toward them over the water, crossed the bridge in front of them, and continued on its way down-stream. Stricken with fear they ran all the way home, where they told of the apparition, and where they swore they'd   never go to that church again — at least not at night.

***

At a place called Catfish Quarry, west of Bedford, two sparkers one night felt a great pressure against the back side of their car. Fleeing as quickly as possible to a place of relative safety, they stopped and shakily examined the back of the car. On the trunk lid they discovered the imprint of a large hand. They later told friends they had tired of Catfish Quarry as a spooning place, and that they would never return there.

***

The alleged rape of a French Lick woman many years ago ended with the hanging from a tree by vigilantes of a man who wore a large hook where his right hand normally would have been.

Years later, while hugging and kissing in a car under that tree one night a young man and his sweetie were startled by the sudden sound of metal scraping on metal and the unexplainable violent rocking of the automobile. They spent little time in speeding away. At the end of their flight they examined the car. Embedded in the hood of the car was a large metal hook, a ringer for the one believed to have been worn by the alleged rapist.

***

On a hill overlooking the French Lick Springs Hotel, vigilantes were said to have hanged a man upside down from a tree until he died. For some time after he died he swayed there, arms outstretched toward the ground.

More than three dozen years later, two lovers in torrid embrace in a car on that hill were interrupted by a scraping sound atop the car. When they got out of the car to investigate, they were greeted by the sight of an upside down hanging body, swinging to and fro, the tips of his marble-hard fingers raking the top of the car.

205

JENNY SIMS

When I met her, Jenny Sims had lived in her house at 606 W. 12th St., in Bloomington a virtual lifetime — sixty years.

She had buried her husband, Melvin, fifteen years earlier on Dec. 27, on their fifty-sixth wedding anniversary, leaving her with a memory of one Christmas season that had stayed as fresh and as clear as yesterday.

They were married in 1926 in the old Massingale residence at Eighth and Rogers streets in Bloomington. If they could come back from where they are now, those few guests who witnessed the marriage ceremony would not recognize the place. Remodeled to new-like condition, it houses a number of offices; quite uptown in appearance.

Though she'd lived in Bloomington those many years, she was a Brown countian born and bred. One of a family of eight children who first saw the light of day in a house along the road about a half mile east of Belmont, she grew up in the care of a mother who raised her children "right."

"When she told me once, I'd better be on the go," Jenny remembered her fondly.

They had a good life together, Jenny and Melvin. He worked thirty-three years at the old Showers furniture factory, now the site of Bloomington's attractive City Hall, and then another seven years at Indiana University.

Barrels of money were not a part of their years together, not even a half barrel. But they had what people used to consider a degree of wealth. They had the essentials — house, home, food on the table and their bills paid. Most of all they had each other. And they got along.

They might have been happier had they had some babies, but they were never blessed in that manner. They loved and wanted them, all right. Even prayed for them. But that was a time when God was fully in charge of people's lives and He didn't send them any. So Jenny did the next best thing that would bring children into their home. She babysat.

For many years she played mother to other people's children, sharing her love with them. Maybe yours, or maybe you are one of those children, and maybe you remember her. Maybe you would not have recognized her when we talked, for she was white-haired then and looking forward to her eighty-ninth birthday.

When she gazed back over the years she lamented, "It's been so long, and there were so many children that I babysat for that I've lost track."

But the memory of her love for them remained.

Although she would have liked to do so, Jenny didn't babysit anymore.

"I can hardly care for myself," she sighed. "I could use the money. Baby sitters get paid as much as a hundred dollars a week now. I am a widow, and my Social Security doesn't go far."

It certainly didn't. One example, and one only, that she and all the elderly face in winter, is the high cost of staying warm. Her December gas bill to heat her four room house was a hundred and seven dollars. She kept the thermostat set at seventy degrees, and she had her favorite chair in front of the furnace blower. The cost of comfort had become punitively costly to the elderly.

Proud, courageous, loving, she took each day as it came. To supplement her monthly Social Security stipend she ironed clothes for other people. Twenty-three men's shirts, nine pairs of pants, and one pair of shorts took her almost six hours. It wasn't the easiest thing, earning money like that. But she was satisfied. The elderly are easily satisfied, God bless them.

Jenny was grateful for friends and neighbors who telephoned, those who provided her with transportation when she needed it, and those who took her to IU basketball games.

"I love the thrill of going to the games," she said of being able to be there in the stands. "I love to see the cheerleaders, and the flags, and the boys."

When I asked her why she didn't find herself a male escort she replied, "I'd probably have to buy him his dinner." And she added, "It's not worth it."

Besides that she had a companion.

Her melodious canary "Billy."

She also had a talking picture of one of her baby sitting days "babies" now grown tall. Given the right touch when her spirits needed a boost, it identified itself by name and the recorded message reminded her that, "I miss you, and I love you very much."

FESTIVAL

To order extra copies of Larry Incollingo's books
please fill out the coupon below and mail to:

REUNION BOOKS
3949 Old SR 446
Bloomington, IN 47401-9747
Phone: 812-336-8403 Fax: 812-336-8599
E-mail: larryi@kiva.net

Please send me:

———— copies of *Festival* @ $12.00 each

———— copies of *The Cottonwood Tree* @ $12.00 each

———— copies of *The Wind Chime Tales* @ $10.50 each

———— copies of *The Tin Can Man* @ $10.50 each

———— copies of *ECHOES of Journeys Past* @$10.50 each

———— copies of *Ol' Sam Payton* @ $9.50 each

———— copies of *Precious Rascal* @ $9.50 each

———— copies of *G'bye My Honey* @ $9.50 each

———— copies of *Laughing All The Way* @ $9.50 each

Add 5% Sales Tax, Plus $2 M&H (up to five books)

_____

NAME

_____

ADDRESS   CITY

_____

STATE   ZIP   TELEPHONE

SEND A GIFT COPY TO A FRIEND

Autograph to:

_____